SAFETY
IN THE
SKIES

BY PERCY KNAUTH

TAB BOOKS Inc.
BLUE RIDGE SUMMIT, PA. 17214

Other TAB books by the author:

No. 2278   *Wind On My Wings*

The excerpt on page 14 is from *The Spirit of St. Louis* by Charles A. Lindbergh. Copyright 1953 by Charles Scribner's Sons. Reprinted with the permission of Charles Scribner's Sons.

The excerpt on page 40 is from *Bonfires to Beacons*, an FAA publication, by Nick A. Komons.

FIRST EDITION

FIRST PRINTING

Library of Congress Cataloging in Publication Data

Knauth, Percy, 1914-
    Safety in the skies.

    Includes index.
    1. Aeronautics—Safety measures. 2. Air traffic
control. I. Title.
TL553.5.K58   1982   363.1'24   82-5938
ISBN 0-8306-2341-8 (pbk.)   AACR2

Cover photo courtesy Les Loman.

Contents

Acknowledgments

This book could not have been written without the help and encouragement of the Federal Aviation Administration (FAA) and some of my pilot friends. I particularly want to thank Nick Komons, Agency Historian, for his help with many historical details; Mike Benson of the FAA Technical Center in Pomona, New Jersey; Manuel Lugris of TRACON, the extraordinary facility that guides every arriving and departing flight into and from New York's three huge airports; and Irv Moss, FAA Information Officer in New York. I also owe immeasurable gratitude to Bill Karraker, now retired from Pan-American Airlines; Bill Strohmeier, formerly of Piper Aircraft; Steve Kenecko of the Danbury School of Aeronautics; and Steve Gentle of Martha's Vineyard, Massachusetts, for helping, advising and teaching me about flying through the years.

Introduction

In this age of the 500-mile-per-hour intercontinental jetliner, with all of its comforts, it may seem anachronistic to publish a book about safety in the skies. After all, with cocktails being served at 40,000 feet and a gourmet dinner bubbling in the galley, who can entertain notions about flying being *un*safe? Statistically, as we all know, it is by far the safest way to travel, and it seems likely that it will get even safer in the years to come.

This isn't a book about lack of safety in flying; on the contrary, it is a book about how flying got to be as safe as it is. It didn't come easy, and there were some milestones of horror along the way. No one who reads here about the Cutting Crash is ever likely to be rid of the picture of a airplane full of passengers flying down a ravine *below* ground level. Anyone who tries to imagine what it was like in 1956 to fall through 20,000 feet of empty sky and *still* have 5,000 feet of the Grand Canyon left to go before hitting the ground will surely have an extra measure of sympathy for the air traffic controllers who prevent such things from happening today.

This story begins at Kitty Hawk, on the Outer Banks of North Carolina, where the first man ever to achieve powered flight took to the air and came down to an uneventful landing. It ends with 1981, the year the Professional Air Traffic Controllers Organization (PATCO) went on strike for better working conditions and better pay. I will leave it to you to decide whether or not they were justified. Their story, as it is told here, may help you to decide.

Between these two events lie some eighty years of patient—and sometimes not so patient—trial and error, argument and counterargument, and endless budgetary wrangles over how to bring safety to the skies. It is absolutely amazing to read how many people thought—and for how long they thought—that this was a relatively unimportant issue. Of course, they didn't fly in airplanes; they wouldn't have done so for anything. But their children do today, and in their children's world, the airplane is the prime carrier.

It is also amazing to realize that at a time when France and Germany were already flying across the South Atlantic, and when England had passenger flights to the Far East, the United States didn't have an airline worthy of the name. Charles Lindbergh made the first nonstop flight from New York to Paris in 1927, but he did it alone, in a single-seat, single-engine airplane that couldn't even have carried a toothbrush with the load of fuel it had on board. It was 27 years before that New York to Paris solo, nonstop flight would be repeated, this time by pilot Max Conrad, the legendary long-distance flier. His airplane was a twin-engine Piper Apache, which he was delivering to a customer in France. Before he got to Paris, an ice storm (Lindbergh braved one too) knocked out his radio and all of his electronic navigation equipment. Thus he flew with the same basic instruments Lindbergh had had: altimeter, turn-and-bank indicator, airspeed indicator, and magnetic compass. That's how young flying was—and still is, even today.

Next time you're outdoors and hear the hum of a passing plane, turn for a second and look at it. There it flies, silvery bright, high in the sky, with its passengers eating or dozing or reading or watching a movie. Somewhere on the ground, a small army of men and women help to keep it aloft with the aid of sophisticated electronic equipment that keeps the crew in constant touch with their protectors. If it's snowing at their landing field, no matter—the plane glides gently and surely to earth, guided by electronic eyes that see through anything.

Orville Wright, who made the first landing in history, may grin in his grave and say: "Well, they may be bigger these days, but basically the procedure's still the same." Basically, it is.

Chapter 1
The First Airways

Twenty-five years ago it was still possible. Private Pilot "X," cartoonist and author, was taxiing his Piper Tripacer toward the head of the active runway at New York's La Guardia Airport when his loudspeaker crackled with a request from Ground Control to move over, stop, and let a DC-7 pass him. The request nettled our hero, a young man with a firm belief in the rights of the individual over those of the shapeless authority of bureaucracy. He kept right on going.

The loudspeaker growled again. "Tripacer so-and-so, please move over to let the DC-7 behind you get by for a priority takeoff." It was the Little Guy against Big Brother, and the Tripacer kept on rolling. It took a third request, this time in peremptory language, to persuade the private pilot that the world was, after all, essentially unfair, and so he moved over.

As the big plane lumbered past him, his glowering eyes took in a startling fact. Stenciled on the nose of the DC-7 was the word *Columbine*. This was not just another overbearing airliner, but yesterday's equivalent of Air Force One: it was President Dwight David Eisenhower's personal airplane.

It is difficult to imagine such a thing happening today; indeed it is quite impossible. With airliners having assumed the main burden of the country's transportation needs, with hundreds of DC-10s, DC-9s, 747s, 727s, L-1011s and other big, complex, and crowded passenger jets preempting the nation's airspace, the small-plane

A Piper Tripacer was asked to move over so the President's plane could make a priority takeoff.

owner in his Piper or his Cessna can hardly get anywhere near one of the major big-city airports—and what's more, doesn't want to. A quarter of a century ago, a quick trip to La Guardia from Spring Valley Airport in New Jersey or nearby Westchester County Airport near White Plains, New York, in a private plane was an attractive proposition: you could just get in your plane and go. You might have to wait your turn to land and you might have to pay some sort of landing fee, but the whole thing was a lot faster, cheaper, and more convenient than taking a train. But, of course, it couldn't last, and it didn't.

Today it is far more than a matter of principle, of equal rights, that rules the skies. When the passenger jet arrived on the scene in the mid-1950s, it changed everything. It wasn't just its speed— more than twice that of piston-engine, propeller-drive airplanes. It wasn't just its size and the number of passengers a single jet could carry. Nor was it just its total reliability in any kind of weather. It was the sum total of all of these things, plus an indefinable something more, that ended the glorious days of freedom in the skies. It was the fact that barely half a century after it was born in Kitty Hawk, the airplane had come of age, had entered its maturity, and had to be reckoned with as a power in its own right in the affairs of the nation. The days of its youth—of uninhibited barnstorming, of landing in cow pastures outside of a town and taking people up for rides at five dollars a throw—were gone forever.

Early fliers were individualists—they *had* to be. Wilbur and Orville Wright were, almost to the point of being antisocial. They just didn't have the time to deal with other people, to let others pry into their business, asking questions, meddling with their affairs. Besides, when they started they didn't know enough to be able to talk about their project to outsiders, even if they had wanted to. Their knowledge was acquired by *doing*. They had to build everything from scratch, even the engine that powered their first airplane. They learned the basics of flight from the birds and from working on a succession of kites and gliders, progressing just a little bit further each time, until, finally, their experience led them into the air.

Most of the early aviators were cast in the same mold. A man had to be practically crazy in order to fly in those days because, for a long time, even assuming that he had somehow acquired a flyable plane, there was nobody around to show him how to fly it. What happened when you got up in the air? He might well wonder, because nobody really knew. The only way to learn was to do it—get up there and find out for yourself. It wasn't safe; of course not. Everyone knew that, and so, for a long time, flight safety was one of the furthest considerations from the minds of those who flew. They knew perfectly well that every time they took off they might

Today, general aviation aircraft transport much of the nation's first class mail.

3

Wilbur and Orville Wright had to build everything from scratch, including the engine and propellers, for the world's first successful airplane.

end up as another statistic—but it might be one that would teach the next man a little bit more.

The basic nature of flying hasn't changed. The air is still an alien element into which we cannot venture without highly specialized equipment. The air is different from water: we can swim in water, or float on it, with just our naked selves for flotation or propulsion. But what about in the air?

Every pilot who has ever learned to fly knows a moment of truth, when the nature of what he is doing is starkly revealed to him. I first experienced this nearly 25 years ago when I was learning to fly with Steve Gentle, the extremely able pilot who ran Katama Airport on the island of Martha's Vineyard, Massachusetts. It was my fourth flight as a student pilot, and we were practicing takeoffs and landings—in other words, getting off the ground and back on it again.

I remember every detail of the moment when the "basic truth" about flying was revealed to me. We were at 800 feet, more or less; it was the standard altitude for the airport flying pattern that would properly line me up for the landing when the time came. It was a cloudy day, with silvery light that cast no shadows. We were over Edgartown Harbor, and below me I could see dozens of pleasure craft tied up to their docks or their moorings, floating absolutely immobile on the dark-green water. Slightly ahead and to my left I could see the hangar and the grass runways of Katama Airport, where I would shortly land. My hands were growing clammy at the thought of what I would have to do before we were safely on the ground again: hold my altitude (which is not as easy as it sounds);

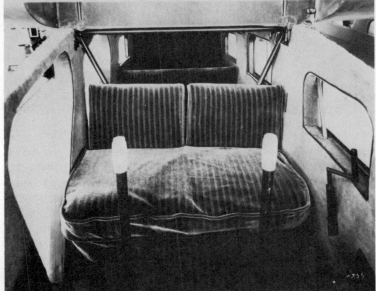

Instrument panel and interior of 1929 four-place Cessna.

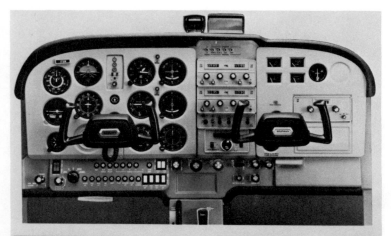

Instrument panel and interior of a modern four-place Cessna.

turn left 90 degrees to my base leg; judge the correct moment to turn another 90 degrees onto my final leg and line up with the runway; cut the throttle to begin our descent; ease on flaps to slow our descent and at the same time give us more lift at the slower speed; clear the telephone wires running across the head of the runway; and, finally, gently set the airplane down.

All of a sudden I didn't want to do any of those things just yet. I had just safely accomplished a takeoff and, more than anything else, I wanted to rest: just a couple of minutes to put back my head, close my eyes, relax, and let my body and mind recover from all the stresses they had just been through. "Why don't I just pull off over there, park and . . . ."

"Pull over and *park*?" my mind screamed at me. Where did I think I *was*, anyway? Before I could park and rest anywhere I first had to get this airplane back on *terra firma*. There was no choice. I had to do all those things I didn't feel like doing right now, and I had to do them at once.

But most important of all, I had to do them *correctly*.

Fortunately, there is an age-old ritual that takes over at a time like this. It is the first thing a fledgling pilot learns when he begins to master that complex and highly important code of behavior that might be called "Manners in the Sky." In the ABCs of flying, this one is Lesson A, and it is called the *pattern*.

It is useful, I have found, to think of flying in terms of three-dimensional geometry. Looking at it in this way, the viewer, be he pilot or passenger, loses that sense of aimlessness that is often so bewildering and frightening to persons venturing aloft for the first time. The sky seems such a huge and empty place; how can one little airplane find its way around up there? The pattern supplies the most important part of the answer by prescribing a set procedure for the most important part of the voyage: coming home.

When he practices takeoffs and landings in seemingly endless sequence at the beginning of his flight training, the student pilot builds the pattern over and over again until, at last, it becomes an ingrained part of him. This is how it goes:

That first moment of truth—I had to land the airplane.

Endlessly practicing takeoffs and landings, the student pilot builds the pattern.

Takeoff: The throttle is pushed home, the engine roars at full power, the plane begins to roll. When lift-off speed is reached, the wheel is eased back gently; the airplane lifts into the sky and becomes airborne. The airplane is now committed to flight: it cannot turn back because a turn would stall the wing, the lifting power would be lost, and the plane would slide off on one wing and crash. It has entered the first phase of the pattern. The pilot climbs to 800 feet above the airport and levels off.

Crosswind leg: Level at 800 feet, the pilot initiates a 90-degree turn to the left. He now has a clear view of the entire airport spread out below on his left side. At this point he announces to the control tower his intention to land and requests a clearance.

Downwind leg: Still in level flight at 800 feet, the pilot makes a second 90-degree turn. Now he is flying parallel to the runway from which he took off, but he is going in the opposite direction, with the wind, if there is any, pushing him along. This is the time to start his checklist for the landing.

Base leg: A 90-degree turn from his downwind leg brings the pilot on to his base leg. This should be well judged so that, when the time comes, he can turn off the base leg and begin his approach to the runway. He will now inform the control tower that he is on base leg and wait for his clearance to land.

Approach leg: A 90-degree turn from his base leg brings the pilot onto his approach leg, and if he has calculated well, he will now be lined up with the runway. The tower has cleared him to land, so he starts his descent. He eases his throttle back and trims the airplane so that it mushes through the air at 85 miles per hour, losing height gradually. He puts on flaps to further kill his speed and to provide extra lift. As the runway begins to flow past beneath his wings, he gently pulls back on the controls, decreasing his speed still further. At the stall speed, with the wheel fully back in his lap, the pilot "feels" for the ground, and then it comes: a soft "choonk-choonk" as the tires touch and start spinning. The flight has ended.

This flight pattern, with local variations, governs takeoffs, approaches, and landings at virtually any airport in the world. Some airports, by reason of their location, may have a right-hand pattern instead of a left-hand one; some may have a short base leg or a short downwind leg. But the basic pattern will be there; the three-dimensional geometry prevails. And for this we can thank the United States Army Air Forces (USAAF) which, during World War II, spread the American system of flying throughout the entire world.

Nor was it an accident that American rules, regulations, and methods of controlling air traffic have been adopted worldwide. It was the American Air Force that first brought aviation to many of the world's more remote areas—and there were few that they missed. In Greenland, for example, such places as Bluie West and Thule were established by the USAAF (as the United States Air Force was known before 1947). The Air Force set up a whole string of bases across Africa to service the Red Ball Express, a superfast supply-delivery line to the remote China-Berma-India theater. The Air Force blasted a runway through a mountain on Ascension Island

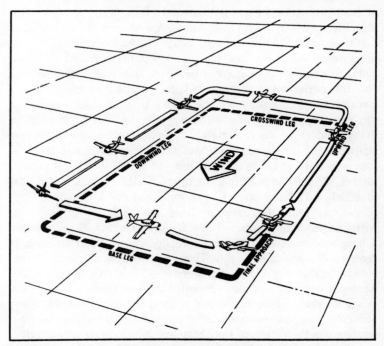

The pattern: crosswind leg, downwind leg, base leg, and final approach.

The Air Force first brought aviation to many of the world's most distant places. Today, from bases in the United States, it can reach any spot on earth within 24 hours. This B-52E is practicing low-level attack over a remote area.

in the South Atlantic, so that converted Liberator bombers could refuel on their way to and from Africa. And all over the tiny—but at that time so vital—islands of the South Pacific there are air strips, now overgrown by the jungles, to testify to the fact that Air Force and U.S. Navy) planes were once based on those far-flung outposts.

But perhaps the greatest tribute to American ability to organize traffic in the skies was the Berlin Airlift of 1948, which beat the Soviet blockade of the four-power capital. For 21 months, in every kind of weather, a steady stream of American and a few British) airplanes carried food, fuel, clothing, and medical supplies—all the necessities of life—to the beleaguered city. A total of 277,569 flights were made by the Berlin Airlift, and in all that time only 12 aircraft and 31 lives were lost due to accident.

Today, more than 30 years later, the discipline of the Berlin Airlift seems almost unbelievable, but if we go back 30 years *before* it happened and look at the background of aviation in America, it seems still more unbelievable. Thirty years *before* the Berlin Airlift puts us at the year World War I ended—1918. At that time there were scarcely any aircraft in America's skies. There was an infant aviation industry turning out deHavilland DH-4s for the war overseas, and there were a few adventurers like Glenn Curtis building airplanes of their design. But there was no air passenger service, and there were no civilian airports anywhere.

10

However, the Air Age in America was being born. When the war ended, the aviators came home. Army surplus airplanes became available, notably the Curtis JN-4 training plane with its fairly reliable OX-5 engine. Known as the "Jenny," this airplane did for aviation what Henry Ford's Model T did for the automobile. The price of a surplus Jenny was such that any pilot who really wanted one could afford it, and once he put his money down, he could fly it away. He didn't even have to show a license because there weren't any.

The Air Age in the United States began as the era of the barnstormer and of the flying circus. All over the country small towns and big cities staged these aerial tournaments, and fliers flocked to them to race, perform stunts, stage mock dogfights, and take up passengers at five dollars per ride. This was about the only way that they could make any money to keep their planes in the air. And so the country gradually became air conscious via the stunt man daredevil. Although it wasn't the best way to promote the idea of safe flying, at least it made the public aware that the airplane was here to stay.

Aviation in the United States, like the country itself, grew haphazardly and without plan. When it did grow, it did so in leaps and spurts, which often pushed it years ahead; but there was no foundation on which the new growth could build. While other nations established airlines and expanded them, Americans were exploring and expanding the new frontiers of the air. They flew the ocean in flying boats, seaplanes equipped with a hull for flotation in 1919,

The barnstormers of the twenties often flew World War I surplus JN-4 "Jennies" fitted with 90-horsepower OX-5 water-cooled engines.

The barnstormers employed daredevil wing-walkers to attract crowds. This one is performing from the spreader-bar of a deHavilland DH-4, a World War I machine also used on the early airmail routes.(Courtesy, Joe R. Reed Collection)

1919, flew nonstop across the continent in 1923, and flew around the world in 1924. They accomplished the first aerial refueling operation in 1923, set a new endurance record of 28 hours 35 minutes in 1925, and reached the North Pole by air in 1926. And then, of course, Lindbergh topped it all with his sensational transatlantic solo flight from New York to Paris in 1927.

All but a few of these things were accomplished without benefit of any government regulations whatsoever. It was not until 1926 that Congress passed the Air Commerce Act, which for the first time established a uniform system of licensing for pilots and aircraft. This act also authorized the creation of a federal airways system, with light and radio beacons to mark major aerial highways. Not that there were any commercial airplanes to use them; that still lay in the future. But the pilots who flew the mails welcomed these beacons: they were useful in turning the hostile dark into something presaging the later friendly skies.

In his book *The Spirit of St. Louis*, Charles A. Lindbergh recalls his days of flying the mail from St. Louis to Chicago. In one passage he describes what the installation of government beacons meant to

Boeing Air Transport flew the mail and a few hardy passengers between Chicago and the West Coast in the Boeing Model 40. It became United Air Lines in December 1928, when Bill Boeing and Fred Rentschler of Pratt & Whitney created America's first big airline. (Courtesy, Boeing Commercial Airplane Company)

the mail pilots: "Eight——nine——ten——eleven——flash. That makes three beacons in sight on the airway ahead—all installed at government expense; by spring our entire airway will be lighted. I subtract fifteen degrees from my heading to cut across the Springfield leg. It's easy to fly by night as by day, with the sky clear, and flashing lights to show me where I am."

Today the airways are marked with very high frequency radio beacons that send out 360 radial beams, one for every degree of the compass rose. These signals are picked up and transcribed by a radio navigational set that translates them into a pointer on an instrument displayed on the compass. All the pilot has to do is to keep the needle centered; he can then unfailingly fly to the next beacon on the airway, where he must reset his radio, pick up a new heading, and fly onward toward his destination. A far cry from the old days indeed!

Chapter 2
The First Airlines

In 1926, the airplane was still a novelty in this country. There were no airlines. There were only a few haphazard air express companies, and these operated on an ad hoc basis. There was no air freight at all. Airmail service was in operation between certain cities, but a few people appreciated what it could really mean to them. Day by day, the mail sacks contained only a fraction of the number of letters they were capable of holding.

Airports were no more advanced, as illustrated by Charles Lindbergh's description of one important airport in 1926:

Lambert Field lies in farming country about ten miles northwest of the St. Louis business district. A pilot, flying high above its sodded acres, sees the Missouri River in the distance, bending north and then east to spew its muddy waters into the clearer Mississippi. The city nestles vaguely in its pall of smoke, a different textured patch contrasting with fields and forests. Southward wooded foothills step up toward the distant Ozark Mountains.

Lambert Field is named after Major Albert Bond Lambert, who commanded a school for balloon pilots during the World War, and who is among the most active leaders in Midwestern aviation. Selected for the site of the National Air Races in 1923, it was enlarged to present size by planking over a little stream which cuts through the eastern end. There are no runways, but the clay sod is good surface for any size of aircraft during summer months. In freezing weather, gusty winds and deepening ruts make operation difficult.

Lambert Field's major commercial activity is carried on by the Robertson Aircraft Company, built and managed by the Robertson brothers, Bill, Frank, and Dan. A little, stove-heated office, two frame warehouses for airplane and engine parts, and half a civilian hangar, house its operations. The corporation's major income results from the sale of reconditioned Army training planes, engines and spares—all placed on the market at extraordinarily low prices.

Airmail pilot Charles Lindbergh sparked a transportation revolution when he flew nonstop from New York to Paris in 1927.

Except on weekends, when the National Guard Squadron comes out in force, one seldom sees more than half a dozen pilots on the field, and the chief activity consists of training students. One can always make a few extra dollars and build up flying time by instructing. Besides, there is no better way of learning the tricks of air and aircraft.

Those of us who instruct know Lambert Field as a child knows the details of his home and yard. We know the erosions on its shallow slope, the downdraft over Anglum, the depressions where drain tiles have caved in. In every azimuth there's a reminder of some past incident of flight. One pushes his plane out of a hangar that housed the Curtis Navy racer. (It left its source of sound somewhere in the air behind as it flashed around the pylons.) At this spot, just beyond the line, George Harmon was killed when his pilot stalled on a left chandelle. (I helped cut him out of the wreckage—unconscious but still alive. He died on the road to the hospital.) Against an east wind, one takes off over the cornfield where Captain Bill spun in after his National Guard Jenny's engine failed. (By some miracle, he wasn't hurt, and climbed out of the crash before we reached him.) There's where Smith and Svengrosh died when they lost a wing in a loop. There's where Frank Robertson and Pres Sultan clipped the top from a big cottonwood tree, without even cracking a spar. (The trunk was eight inches in diameter where their Jenny snapped it off.) On the side of that ditch is where Bud Gurney broke his arm in a parachute spot-landing contest. The pigpen by the white farmhouse is where O.E. Scott once nosed over.

How Scotty loved to tell that story! His engine cut on take-off. He wasn't high enough to turn. Straight ahead lay the pigpen, and in it he landed. Muck caught his wheels and whipped him upside down. He found himself hanging in his safety belt, his head two or three feet above a stinking wallow, "with all those pigs squealing and nudging in around me, just as though I was one of 'em!"

As commercial aviation developed in the 1920s the United States was not even in the running. The land where the first airplane

15

flew (the very land that was to bring forth the DC-3 transport and the Boeing 747 jumbo jet) had few passenger planes in 1926. The United States had no aviation regulations; there was no aviation law. In Europe, airports like Croydon in England, Le Bourget in Paris, and Tempelhof in Berlin were way stations on flights that spanned whole continents. Some airliners carried as many as fourteen passengers. What was wrong, then, with aviation in America?

It is a complex story, one that is not told simply. Involved were service rivalry in the armed forces; political rivalry; and reluctance on the part of businessmen to invest large sums of money in a product of whose reliability they remained unconvinced. One common denominator that ran through all the tangle and hampered the growth of aviation in the United States was money.

In Europe the airlines received government subsidies for carrying the mail. With this kind of support they were able to extend their airmail and passenger services, until, at last, Germany and France were carrying airmail across the South Atlantic to Argentina and Brazil. In January, 1923 Britain appointed the Civil Air Transport Committee, which allocated one million pounds of government money to help the airlines. An immediate result was the formation of Imperial Airways, a national carrier that eventually incorporated all the British airlines and initiated a service linking Britain with the most distant lands of its Empire.

The Post Office pioneered the domestic airmail routes in the United States. During the early twenties equipment was mostly war surplus DH-4s fitted with 400-horsepower Liberty engines.

The Liberty-powered Ford-Stout 2-AT was predecessor of the legendary Ford Trimotor. Florida Airways, organized in 1926, was soon gobbled up by Pan Am.

In 1926 America had nothing to compare even remotely with this. The intermediate fields at which Lindbergh landed when carrying the mail from St. Louis to Chicago were nothing more than designated cow pastures. At night a row of lanterns was hung along a fence to indicate where he should land; sometimes the headlights of a car would be aimed down his landing strip. Lindbergh recalls one instance when, on a foggy night, he was saved by a homemade beacon put up by a boy to help the mail pilots who nightly flew over his house. The "beacon" was a lamp with a 100-watt bulb.

The Airmail Act of 1925, which President Calvin Coolidge signed into law, finally began to put an end to this chaotic state of affairs in the American skies. When the Kelly Act, as it was called (named after its sponsor, Representative Clyde Kelly of Pennsylvania) became law, it enabled the Post Office to contract the services of commercial air carriers for the delivery of domestic mail. Since there were virtually no commercial carriers at the time, this was an immediate incentive to businessmen to get in their and start some.

Nobody mentioned it at the time, but this was also the moment at which the idea of legislating safety in the air first began to take hold. It may be difficult to believe, but at this time anybody could fly simply by buying an airplane, new or used, cranking up the engine, getting in, and flying away. It didn't matter whether or not the owner knew *how* to fly. If he didn't, he either learned quickly or died quickly. If he did, there was no one around to determine how well he

17

flew. Nor was there any authority to inspect the aircraft or the engine, to note how long each had been used, or to certify the aircraft for use with or without passengers. There was simply no regulation at all.

Quietly, but almost immediately, the Kelly Act began to change all this. First, business began to get into the flying game—and it wasn't just fly-by-night business either. Within two months after the act became law, the postmaster general received more than 2,000 inquiries from businessmen asking how they could qualify for airmail contracts. Among these were William Rockefeller, Cornelius Vanderbilt Whitney, Philip K. Wrigley, Lester Armour, Charles F. Kettering, Marshall Field, and Robert P. Lamont. Rockefeller and Whitney invested in National Air Transport (NAT), later absorbed by United Airlines and just to make sure, they also put money into Colonial Airlines, later absorbed by American Airlines. Thus two big carriers got started almost immediately and set the tone for developing American air transport for many years to come.

William "Jacknife" Stout and his Ford Trimotor airplane. Stout interested Henry and Edsel Ford in aviation. (Don Dwiggins Photo)

Henry Ford (facing camera) invested heavily in civil aviation following passage of the 1925 Kelly Act. He helped attract other significant sources of capital to the infant industry.

One of the most sensational entrants was Henry Ford, who came complete not only with money but also with an airplane. Actually, he had been developing the famous "Tin Goose" since 1923, when he had bailed out William Bushnell Stout, producer of a large, trimotor, all-metal monoplane. Nearly 60 years later several examples of the Tin Goose, which had excellent short-field characteristics, are still flying, remarkable testimony to the quality of its construction.

When contracts were awarded, Ford got two mail routes: Detroit-Cleveland and Detroit-Chicago. Colonial got Boston-New York; National Air Transport got Chicago-Dallas. These were the first contracts; still in the offing were the transcontinental routes.

By late 1926 there were more than 40 airline operators in the United States, a figure that is misleading because it sounds bigger than it actually was. The greater proportion of these were small companies—some with only a few airplanes—struggling to grow so that they could reap their share of the profits to be made in aviation. Their presence on the scene made the United States airway map a crazy quilt of lines that quite often seemed to go from nowhere to nowhere, and this certainly held forth little promise for an orderly growth of aviation in the land that gave it birth.

The solution to this problem became the goal of Walter Folger Brown, friend of President Herbert Hoover. Hoover had name him postmaster general, and in the power to distribute the airmail subsidies Brown saw just the tool he needed for remaking the nation's helter-skelter airway system into something coherent and manageable. And this he proceeded to do in a manner that at times approached the dictatorial but that, in the end, gave the United States a modern, forward-looking airways system and, eventually, aviation regulations it so badly needed.

Brown's strongest conviction was that there was no point in

President Hoover's postmaster general, Walter Folger Brown, structured the American domestic airline system using his mail-pay whip.

A Douglas M-2 mail plane operated by Western Air Express. Postmaster General Brown would force the merger of WAE and Transcontinental Air Transport to form TWA (originally called Transcontinental & Western Air; and later, Trans World Airlines).

dealing with the many small, fly-by-night operators whose routes led from Podunk to Golliwash and who were now trying to cash in on some of the bigger profits aviation promised via the subsidy route. America's future, he contended, lay with the strong, and so it was the strong with whom he dealt, even if it involved such crude methods as simply not inviting the small-time operators to meetings.

Another tool Brown proposed to use was the Watres Act which, when signed into law by Hoover in April, 1930, brought about certain changes in the manner in which airmail subsidies were paid. The principal one was a change from a rate per pound of mail carried to a rate of space per mile, to be paid regardless of how much cargo was being carried. This meant that, among other things, the airlines would be investing in larger airplanes with more space to carry mail—and also more space to carry passengers.

Armed with the Watres Act, Brown had, in effect, dictatorial powers over commercial aviation, and he had no hesitation about using them. He was looking ahead now to the establishment of transcontinental airline routes. As he saw it, there should be three: one northern line, one central, and one southern. Then there would be transverse routes running north and south, with feeder lines in between.

The story of how this vision was finally achieved is one full of the most dubious dealings, pressures, and subterfuges which, at times, came very close to crossing the borderline of law. One of the most controversial was a provision, introduced by Brown, that an airline, in order to submit an acceptable bid, must show proof of at least six months' experience in operating aircraft on regular night schedules over a route of 250 miles or more. This was the kind of experience most of the independents did not have, since they had never needed it; in fact, about the only ones who could show such proof were airmail operators. The result was—as Brown had intended it to be—that small airlines were eliminated at the very start.

Not all of them took it lying down. The president of United States Airways, N. A. Letson, whose line ran between Kansas City and Denver, merged with two other small-time operators and submitted a bid for the central line under the new name of United Avigation Company. He hung on tenaciously until Brown finally got him out of the running by persuading American Airways, which became American Airlines in 1929, to sublet to Letson an airmail route running from Kansas City to Denver. Others were eliminated by being bought up outright by some of the big operators, or they were simply squeezed to the wall.

America's first scheduled overseas airline was Pan American Airways and this Fokker Trimotor was part of the Pan Am fleet during the late twenties.

A popular private airplane of the early thirties was the Great Lakes Sport, an open-cockpit biplane powered by the 90-horsepower Cirrus engine. The first reliable and economical lightplane engine was the 40-horsepower Continental which appeared in the mid-thirties. The Continental and Lycoming lightplane engines in use today are all descended from the lowly Continental A-40.

Whatever his methods, Brown got what he wanted, and by the end of the Hoover administration, the United States was a true aviation power, with double the airways route mileage—close to 30,000 miles—that had existed when Brown started reshaping his airways map. The three transcontinental routes were an established fact, with United, American, TWA, and Eastern the principal beneficiaries. North and south, the country was served by Eastern Air Transport on the east coast, United from Chicago to Dallas, and United again along the west coast. Most of America's major transportation centers now had air transport serving them, and by 1932 nearly half a million passengers were taking advantage of the new service. Air transport had arrived for good; the stage was now set to make it safe and reliable.

Chapter 3
Growing Pains

Now that the United States had an air transport system, it remained to convince the public that airplanes were safe to fly in and that the time saving they represented was real and not going to be eaten up by diversions because of weather, unreliable aircraft, or accidents. During the mid-1920s, when Postmaster General Brown was starting his campaign to reshape the airways map and start the aviation industry on its way, these fears were very real. Most of the airplanes that Americans knew were barnstorming and flying-circus craft, hardly the sort that would inspire the confidence of sober-minded businessmen making comparisons between airplanes and railroad trains.

In May, 1927, something dramatically changed all that. Seldom in history can one point to the single deed of a single man and say: "This was a turning point that changed the world"; but in this case the statement is justifiable. The man was Charles Lindbergh, an obscure airmail pilot flying for the Robertson Line out of St. Louis, and the event was his solo flight across the Atlantic Ocean, nonstop from New York to Paris.

It is important to point out that Lindbergh's flight was made in an airplane designed to an American, built in an American factory (the Ran plant in San Diego, California), and powered by an American-designed and American-built engine, the Wright Whirlwind. Others were trying to accomplish the same feat—there was a $25,000 prize attached to it—but in many cases the names of the pilots betrayed their foreign origins, and most of the airplanes involved were foreign built. Not one of the other contenders showed the same faith in the American aviation industry that Lindbergh did when he opted to fly a domestic single-engine plane. A great many people thought he was crazy, but he had reasons for his choice: a single power plane, well built and tested, meant there was that much less chance for trouble. And he was proved to be triumphantly right.

More than anything else possibly could have, Lindbergh's flight dramatized the reliability of a well-built, well-maintained airplane. About the only similarity between the *Spirit of St. Louis* and the kind of airplanes Americans were accustomed to seeing in 1927 was that each had wings and a propeller. But there the similarity ended. The *Spirit of St. Louis* seemed a light and slender aircraft as it stood on the runway, surprisingly "clean" aerodynamically. Yet on that May morning when it took off for Paris, it lifted one of the greatest loads ever carried into the air by a plane of its size—and this from a field that was soggy with rain.

At that time there were two principal types of airplanes flying in the United States. Most of them were biplanes with two wings one above the other. The other types were monoplanes, the transports and load-carriers: the trimotor Fokker, the trimotor Ford-Stout "Tin Goose," and others of the same general concept. Com-

By the time President Roosevelt took office in 1933, the United States had the world's best domestic airline system.

25

pared to the light and slender *Spirit of St. Louis,* these heavy cumbersome, and hard-to-handle aircraft seemed like dinosaurs.

By the time Franklin Delano Roosevelt became President in 1933, the air transport picture in America had changed dramatically. Within just six years of the passing of the Kelly Act in 1925, one American airport—Newark, in the New Jersey meadowlands across the Hudson from New York—had alone outpaced the combined total of Croydon, Le Bourget, and Tempelhof, the largest and busiest European airports, in its number of operations. Los Angeles, Chicago, and Philadelphia were all busier than the busiest European airports. United Airlines, America's biggest carrier, was transporting more than half again as many passengers as Lufthansa German Airlines, the largest European carrier. Pan American Airways was flying more multiengine transports than all of Europe's airlines put together. In the aviation industry, the United States had moved, in one jump, to the forefront.

Money and the fact that they could make a profit on airmail and subsidized passenger transport were in no small measure responsible for this sudden growth on the part of the airlines, but another very important factor had also begun to contribute its share. A new industry was about to be born—an industry in which the United States would seize and hold supremacy for the next half century. The American aircraft manufacturing industry, for years as moribund as aviation itself, was about to flex its muscles and start moving.

In the early 1930s, the most important mode of transport in the United States was the railroad—but the railroad was finite in its capabilities. In 1932 it still took four days to travel from New York to California, and that seemed as fast as anybody would ever be likely to go. Up to that time the airplane had not been able to do better: refueling stops, weather hazards, crew changes, and overnight stops all combined to make cross-country air travel at least as tedious as and a good deal less comfortable than the train.

But now things were about to happen. The airlines, knowing they could do better if they only had the airplanes, were pressing the industry to get them out of the dinosaur age and into something more modern—something that would enable them to compete on equal terms with the railroads. And in the early 1930s, they began to get it.

Three leaders in aircraft manufacture began to emerge: Boeing, Douglas, and Lockheed. They were the Ford, General Motors, and Chrysler of the industry, and, they have held the positions of

The Douglas DC-1 was delivered to TWA in 1933. Only one was built, but it fathered the DC-2, which followed a year later, and the venerable DC-3; which evolved by 1936.

leadership that they established in those years ever since. Each of them, in response to the same urgency from the airlines, produced a new airplane that at last broke the World War I shackles, which had fettered the industry for so long. Boeing produced the B-247 for its major client, United Airlines. Lockheed produced the Electra. Douglas produced the DC-1, which very quickly evolved into the most famous and most useful transport plane in history: the Douglas DC-3.

It was significant that all of these airplanes looked basically alike. All three had dropped the biplane wings. All three had abandoned the boxy designs of their forerunners and showed clean, smoothly curved, aerodynamically efficient fuselage construction. All three were all-metal. And all three had thick, cantilevered wings that thrust outward from the lower side of the fuselage and carried on them not three, but two smoothly cowled, radial, air-cooled engines. Gone was the big, uncowled, radial engine located in the nose, whirling its propeller right in front of the pilot's face. These airplanes looked as though they could slip through the air as easily as a raindrop—and they did.

The history of American aviation is full of paradoxes, and not the last of these is the history of the next few years, when the industry began to realize its potential for the first time. These were

27

the blackest years of the Depression, when business in the country seemed to have come to a standstill; when unemployment reached 23.6 percent in 1932; when agricultural prices had reached such disastrous levels that farmers were slaughtering their livestock and pouring fresh milk into ditches. It was scarcely a promising time for an entire new industry to start turning out product, yet the aviation construction business was one of the few growth industries in the country from the beginning.

It began with the Boeing 247. United Airlines, like the other airlines, had been pressing for new and more efficient aircraft, and the B-247, first off the line, was Boeing's answer. Early on, however, it revealed a major flaw: it was designed to carry only 10 passengers. This gave an unexpected opening to Donald Douglas, who was designing a similar airplane for TWA. His prototype, the DC-1, was designed to carry 14 people, and because Douglas used the new, high-powered Wright Cyclone engine rather than the lower-powered Pratt & Whitney Wasp, which United had specified for the Boeing 247, it was able to carry that number. Further, it could match the 160-miles-per-hour cruising speed of the B-247, crossing the continent in 19¾ hours, and this at a lower operating cost.

Thus began the development of what is probably the most famous transport plane in history. The DC-1, which was immediately in great demand, led quickly to the DC-2. The DC-2, in turn, led to something radically, the DC-3: The Douglas Sleeper Transport (DST), as it was called, was essentially a DC-2 modified to accept sleeping berths. Now TWA could not only offer a transcontinental trip in one-quarter the time it took by train, it could also match the train's sleeping comfort as well.

However, it was not the sleeping berth that brought the DC-3 its lasting fame. When it was used as a daytime air transport, it could accommodate 21 passengers in its widened fuselage. This just about put the Boeing 247 out of business and made the DC-3 the most beloved airplane in American skies. After the bombing of Pearl Harbor, it became the most favored transport plane of World War II. Even today, almost half a century after it was first built, it is still used in many parts of the world, including the United States, where it is occasionally seen performing as a luxury executive plane.

The third of the new trio of modern air transports was the Lockheed Electra. It carried 10 passengers and was powered with two Pratt & Whitney Wasp Junior engines. With a top speed of 203 miles per hour, it was the fastest of the three, but its principal importance is that it laid the groundwork for a long line of notable Lockheed airplanes, beginning with the 12 and 14 and including that famous workhorse of the postwar years, the Lockheed Constellation.

With these three aircraft, aviation grew up in America. It was now possible to set up regular schedules and adhere to them. This, together with speed, at last gave the airplane the competitive advantage it needed over the railroad. The result was a burgeoning of traffic, which put aviation in a whole new light. In 1930, there were 85,125,000 passenger-miles flown, and two years after that the number was 127,433,000. In the same amount of time, the number of passengers carried tripled. Further more, in three years' time aviation increased its work force by 254 percent, even though workers in other industries were being let go all over the country. Air transport, it seemed, was the only depression-proof industry in the country.

Federal regulation, however, was a long time in coming and its development had to follow a tortuous road. It must be remembered that there were absolutely no precedents to follow here: aviation and its regulation had never existed before. And before we go into the details of how regulation was finally achieved and what it accomplished, perhaps it would be instructive to recount a little story that was typical of the thinking of the time.

Almost half a century later, DC-3s are still at work around the world. (Photo by R. Besecker)

The Lockheed Constellation was ordered by TWA and Pan Am prior to World War II, but only 15 were built before war's end, all going to the military. (Photo courtesy Pan American World Airways)

The story begins, in a way, with the Public Works Administration (PWA), Roosevelt's brainstorm for providing work for the unemployed by giving them public works to do. One of the projects agreed upon was improving existing airports or building new ones, and by the winter of 1933-34 some 70,000 men were working at 700 airports, existing or new, around the country. It was felt that such a program would not only improve the existing situation for flying but would also enhance the possibilities for a broadened flying program, since many of the new fields could service communities that, at the time, had no way of gaining access to the nation's air network.

At this time Eugene Vidal, chief of the Bureau of Air Commerce, expressed some thoughts on aviation's "forgotten man" to the Society of Automotive Engineers. Himself a flier, Vidal said:

The forgotten man of aviation is the private flier, and his brothers are legion. They work at manual training branches in high schools and at engineering tables in colleges, and each dreams of the day when his inspired design will revolutionize aeronautics. They build model airplanes by the millions and trudge out to local airports each weekend to worship their idols from the ground and long for the day when they will have saved enough to buy a hop. They are the young business women and men who travel by air and would like to fly for recreation or sport or pleasure but cannot afford to. They are the older folks, who would like to include air travel in their daily social and business lives but have not yet met it within the ken of their experiences. They are the multitudes who admire Lindbergh . . . and all others to whom the air is as commonplace as Sunday roads, but stand on the edge longingly—physically and mentally worthy of the kingdom of flight, but financially unprepared.

The point of all this rhetoric was that Vidal wanted to democratize aviation, to give the masses some sort of "flivver" plane. In today's age of skies aswarm with Cessnas and Pipers and Beechcraft and Mooneys along with 747s, 727s, DC-10s, Lockheed L-1011s, and all the other myraid flying machines to which we have fallen heir, it may seem incredibly naive of the nation's chief aviation officer to be talking and thinking in this way; but it is a good illustration of the way the people felt in those times and what a long reach in imagination they had to make to come up with anything sensible in the way of regulating aviation. For in truth, Vidal's idea did not die with that speech: it lived on and came close to reality.

For one thing, the feeling was that it might be a way to help revive the general aviation industry, which was hard-hit by the Depression: civil aircraft production was down from 5,414 units in 1929 to 896 in 1932, while all aeronautical products together dropped from $91 million to $34.8 million. Flying schools were also suffering, with enrollments barely more than half what they had been in 1929.

If the flivver plane could be realized, it might help this situation. It should be low-priced and easily operated and maintained, said Vidal, and it must be produced and sold in large numbers. Henry Ford, as early as 1924, had said that there was no reason airplanes could not be mass-produced, and Vidal, studying the question, finally decided that for $700 a customer could have a two-seat, single-engine plane that could fly 100 miles per hour. Consultation with Ford engineers at Dearborn, Michigan, brought an estimate of $65 for a converted automobile engine, provided a full day's production of 3,500 units were purchased.

The Waco QFC was typical of private aircraft of the thirties. (Photo by Bill Selikoff)

The Cessna EC-3 appeared during the early thirties, but it was not successful.

Vidal got Roosevelt's approval for the plan and even got a promise of $1 million for start-up costs, which, however, was cut down to $500,000 in negotiations with the PWA; but this did not seem to bother Vidal. The sum, he said, was still sufficient to launch the flivver plane project.

Vidal even went so far as to conduct a market survey; this

Many home-built airplanes took to the skies during the late twenties and early thirties fitted with motorcycle and automobile engines. This one was powered with a Model A Ford engine.

Eugene Vidal's dream of a mass-produced "flivver" plane that would be within the financial research of everyone was unrealistic. No such market ever existed. But today, the amateur-built plane movement, organized as the Experimental Aircraft Association (EAA) and well regulated, counts more than 60,000 active members, most of whom attend the annual EAA Fly-In/Convention at Oshkosh, Wisconsin. (Photo by Don Downie)

survey further demonstrated how much ignorance still existed among the general population on the subject of flying. Of 18,000 replies received to his February, 1934, questionnaire, 13,000 said they would buy the airplane when it came on the market. They also listed 57,000 additional possible purchasers; friends who were said to be good prospects. These figures led Vidal to the optimistic conclusion that probably one in ten of this group could be considered a purchaser.

However, nothing ever came of this program, primarily because no suitable engine was available and because market did not actually exist.

Chapter 4
Communications Gap

On May 6, 1935, TWA Flight 6, bound from Los Angeles to New York via Albuquerque, Kansas City, Columbus, and Pittsburgh, lifted off the runway at Los Angeles, turned east, and headed for its first stop. Passengers settling back in their seats saw no reason to expect anything other than a routine, although long, flight. The plane reached Albuquerque, refueled, and took off again, bound now for Kansas City. About 100 miles out of the Kansas City Airport, however, things began to go sour.

For one thing, the airplane ran into rainy weather and the pilot had to go on instruments. For another thing, he discovered that his radio was acting up and he was having difficulty staying in two-way contact with the ground, an absolute must for instrument flight. Finally, and most alarming, he received a weather broadcast informing him that the ceiling at Kansas City Airport was 600 feet. Since the landing minimum was 700 feet, this ruled out Kansas City as a stop unless the weather lifted.

There were, of course, other options. The flight could head for Wichita or Omaha, both of which reported clear skies, and refuel there. Or the pilot could climb above the weather, overfly Kansas City, and land at Burlington, Iowa, or at Kirksville, Missouri, both of which lay along the route and were available for refueling.

Nobody knows why the pilot of TWA Flight 6 chose to ignore all these attractive possibilities and decided to try landing at Kansas City anyway. This meant an extremely careful flight along the radio range that was lined up with his landing runway and then a delicate and dangerous descent until he could see the ground below that 600-foot ceiling and set the airplane down visually. Unfortunately, there were a number of things that could go wrong with such a procedure, and in this case most of them did.

For one thing, there was another TWA flight ahead of him also trying to get into Kansas City. This flight had taken off from Los Angeles half an hour ahead of Flight 6 and so had arrived at Kansas City just before the weather went below minimums. But it was now having difficulty landing, and altogether made three attempts before getting down safely. Meanwhile Flight 6 had to wait its turn, and instead of sending it on to another field as prudence dictated he should, the TWA flight dispatcher kept the airplane circling. Then, when he tried to raise the pilot on the radio to tell him to come in, he got no answer to his repeated radio calls.

What happened? It took a long, drawn-out, and bitter investigation, including one by a congressional committee, to get what appeared to be the most likely story. The pilot of Flight 6 had circled Kansas City until he dared circle no longer—he was afraid he would run short of fuel while attempting the difficult landing. He had then decided, belatedly, to head for Kirksville, the nearest field and one that was in easy reach. About 16 miles away, in order to be sure not to miss it, he had brought his airliner down to minimum altitude, at times flying below the tops of the trees. In doing so, he had inadvertently descended into a wide ravine, or draw, and when he reached the end of the draw, he didn't have time to pull the airplane up out of it. It crashed, at full speed, below ground level.

This crash marked a turning point in American aviation history. It has become known as the Cutting Crash because one of the victims was United States Senator Bronson M. Cutting, a Republican from New Mexico. Furthermore, Cutting, an early supporter of President Roosevelt and the New Deal, was at the time a controversial man. He had broken with Roosevelt over the reduction of veterans' pensions and, as a result, the president had supported his opponent, Denis Chavez, in the 1934 elections. Cutting had won a very narrow victory which Chavez, on Roosevelt's advice, disputed.

The Cutting Crash, therefore, came in for far more than its expectable share of attention. Blame was at first attached to the pilot, the copilot, and the dispatcher, but TWA rejected this finding and instead blamed the Bureau of Air Commerce (BAC). The congressional investigation became so mired down in politics that its report made little sense, and the Bureau of Air Commerce found

In the thirties, airframe testing standards were still largely empirical. The strength of the horizontal stabilizer and elevator of this Great Lakes biplane was tested with a load of sandbags. "Eyeball" engineering, however, often resulted in airframes of greater strength than necessary.

itself in the intolerable position of investigating itself and also of defending itself against an irate airline. In short, the Cutting Crash brought out just about everything that was wrong with Roosevelt's aviation policy—and much was wrong.

Meanwhile, airplanes kept on flying, and, particularly around the terminals, matters got worse. One reason for this was not a surfeit of airplanes but a deficit of personnel. The Bureau of the Budget did nothing to help matters here: year by year, in line with the administration's economy drive, it cut the funds available for regulating commercial air traffic. In May, 1936, there were just 60 men to carry out the Bureau of Air Commerce's inspection functions; awaiting inspection were 14,000 licensed fliers, 24,000 student pilots, 8,000 aircraft, and 2,500 mechanics. And the money allotted the bureau to do its job was $0.644 million.

Safety figures reflected the situation. In 1936 the passenger fatality rate doubled to 10.1 per 100 million passenger miles flown; the Airline Pilots Association has calculated that, on the average, one air carrier pilot was killed every 28 days. Public mistrust of air travel hit an all-time low. And yet, for all of the unease, for all of the mounting sense of disaster, nobody really knew what to do.

Reed Airline, which flew six-place Travel Airs between Wichita Falls, Texas, and Oklahoma City during the early thirties, was typical of the many small operators of that period who began feeder routes but were doomed to failure without a mail-pay subsidy.

Help came from a totally unexpected quarter. Royal S. Copeland, head of the congressional committee that had investigated the Cutting Crash, released a preliminary report of the committee's findings; it was so obviously distorted, so unfair, so politically motivated that it brought matters to a head. "Hot on the trail of Senator Copeland's condemnation of the Bureau of Air Commerce," wrote *Business Week* in July, 1936, "comes the news that the government is taking over active control of air traffic." And so

During the Great Depression the small operators offered fares that were close to those charged by the bus lines. The Wichita Falls-Oklahoma City round trip was $12 for a total distance of 280 miles.

indeed it was. The federal government had finally opened its eyes to what had for so long been so obvious: aviation needed regulating, and aviation—or at least large segments of it—knew it and demanded it. And the first place that regulations had to be put into effect was in the terminal areas.

From the perspective of 50 years later, it is difficult to understand today why the major air terminals of the nation were not littered with the wreckage of aircraft and the smashed bodies of dead passengers in the early 1930s. Places like Newark, Lambert Municipal in St. Louis, Hoover Field in Washington, and Cleveland Municipal used light guns to advise incoming pilots whether they were cleared to land. And yet airports like these were handling between 50 and 60 landings and departures per hour in peak periods, with no voice communication whatsoever with the arriving or departing aircraft. Furthermore, the traffic arrived completely at random, not in an orderly flow, since there was no airways traffic control to sort it out as it approached the airport. So the only way the controllers knew an airplane was coming in was when they saw it, by which time they might well be trying to keep three or four other aircraft from colliding. And just to make matters worse, the pilots were on their mettle to get onto the runway and into the terminal as quickly as they could, lest they be held up and have to circle, thus delaying their passengers. So cooperation from them was usually forthcoming only when danger was so imminent that it could not be ignored.

One answer was obvious: to establish control via radio. Cleveland Municipal was the first place to introduce this, along with the construction of the first prototype of a modern control tower. The tower was built high so that incoming airplanes could be clearly seen, and it was located in a spot that gave an unobstructed view in all directions. But most important, it possessed a radio antenna and a radio to go with it. The traffic controller was therefore able to contact an incoming flight, to provide information on the weather, on landing conditions, and on the presence of other aircraft, and, finally, to give clearance for landing. And the same sort of control could be exercised over aircraft preparing to take off.

Such was the fruit borne of the uneasiness and fear that were gradually spreading over the nation on the subject of safety in the air. Instrument flying, now becoming a common cure for the ills of bad weather, was contributing to the problems and was making voice contact between airplanes as well as between airplanes and the ground even more important. Groping around in fog, rain, or snow over an airport, airplanes were so vulnerable to collision that, in a kind of black humor, jokes about them even got into congressional hearings. Since congressmen were so dependent on the airplane, these were not received with laughter but with grim warnings that something had better be done.

The first thing that was done was to restrict private flying in instrument weather from the vicinity of airways radio beams or air carrier airports. Predictably, there was a howl of protest. But there was really no choice—something had to give and the private fliers, being the most vulnerable, were the ones who had to give. And, just as it is today, number of near-misses—but fortunately no midair collisions—forced the issue.

The next step was to organize all interested parties—civil, military, airline, and federal—to meet and discuss ways and means of instituting effective traffic control. The occasion was extraordinary: nothing like this had ever been done before, there were no precedents, no guidelines. And there was no money and no time: budget appropriations for funds to set up a new system would take months, and winter, with its greatly increased demand for instrument flying, was only weeks away.

Once again, there wasn't much choice. It was a foregone conclusion that eventually the government would run the traffic control

The Travel Air Model 6000, operated on several feeder routes, was fitted with a 300-horsepower Wright Whirlwind engine. The Travel Air Company was founded in Wichita, Kansas, in 1925 by Clyde Cessna, Lloyd Stearman, and Walter Beech; it became a Curtiss-Wright subsidiary in 1929.

system, but meanwhile the government—in the form of the Bureau for Air Commerce—was in no position to do so. Eugene Vidal, the head of the BAC, therefore made the extraordinary proposal that the airlines set up the system and run it for the next 90 to 120 days, after which the BAC would take over. The airlines agreed.

Thus it happened that four airlines—United, American, Eastern, and TWA—set up the first experimental air traffic control unit at Newark Airport, controlling the traffic on the Newark-Cleveland-Chicago route. Simultaneously, the ban on private fliers was relaxed, providing they filed flight plans with the BAC and with at least one airline flying the route they planned to use.

Nick A. Komons, official historian of the Federal Aviation Administration, has left us a graphic picture of how these first attempts at airways traffic control were set up and how they functioned. It shows how extraordinarily well those early planners solved their horrendous problems and how direct is the line that leads from those early beginnings of nearly half a century ago to the computerized facilities that help airliners into airports today. In his book, *Bonfires to Beacons*, Komons describes the situation:

Each station was manned by a crew of five—a manager, assistant manager, and three controllers. The stations operated 16 hours a day, from 8 A.M. to midnight; but the availability of air traffic control services itself created more traffic and the stations eventually went on a 24-hour schedule. The crews worked overlapping shifts. The largest on-duty contingent, present during periods of heaviest traffic, numbered three; the smallest, one.

Each station was equipped with a blackboard, a large table map, a teletype machine, and a telephone.

Flights were posted on the blackboard, which detailed their progress and their estimated time of arrival and altitude over designated geographical fixes. The information on the board was transferred to the map, on which all airways were plainly marked. Small brass markers shaped like shrimp boats, one for each flight in the control area, dotted the map. Each marker was equipped with a clip, to which could be attached a slip of paper. The controller noted on the paper the name of the airline, the flight number, the flight's time of departure, and cruising altitude. Placed in positions on the map corresponding to the actual flight progress of aircraft, these markers showed by their pointed ends the direction of flight and gave a clear, concise picture of what would probably take place as incoming aircraft converged around the terminal area. Each marker was moved every 15 minutes to conform to the actual or estimated progress made by the aircraft.

When there controllers were on duty, each performed a distinct function. The so-called "A" controller issued all necessary instructions to aircraft, including clearances, and maintained the dispatch board and the inbound flight log. The "B" controller, or coordinator, handled the weather sequences, maintained two other logs and positioned the shrimp boats on the map. The "C" controller, or calculator, calculated the speed of incoming ships, estimated the time they would arrive over designated fixes, and entered these estimates on the blackboard. During periods of low traffic activity, one man performed all three functions. When two men were on duty, the functions of the coordinator were split.

Only passive control was exercised over aircraft flying in controlled areas during good weather. Nevertheless, their progress was followed as if they were under active control, and pilots were informed of other aircraft within 15 minutes or less of their line of flight and of the estimated time and altitude these aircraft would pass over designated points.

Aircraft came under active control only during instrument flight. When ATC [Air Traffic Control] was under airline jurisdiction, its function was to keep en route airline traffic separated and flowing in such a manner that it arrived at terminal areas in orderly sequence. The Bureau recognized that under its jurisdiction airway control had to be expanded to include all aircraft flying the civil airways on instrument. "We have been prone, perhaps subconsciously, to think of airline transports when air traffic control is mentioned," Earl Ward cautioned. "However, the safety of passengers in and operations of other than scheduled air transports must be given consideration. An air transport can be jeopardized by lack of supervised control of an operator of any other aircraft . . .." Safety required that all instrument flights "proceed from origin to destination in a prescribed manner."

This was the groundwork for what evolved into the present-day sophisticated airways control system with its very-high-frequency omnirange (VOR) beacons, its en route radar, and its two-way very high frequency (VHF) communication between planes in the air and planes on the ground. Everything that was added was improved equipment—devices like the transponder, the distance-measured equipment, and, above all, the constantly improved radar.

And, finally, the rules were codified. In August, 1936, regulations were issued governing instrument flight. Equipment was specified for the airplane: two-way radio and a prescribed set of instruments for maintaining precision flight control. The airplane had to be specifically licensed for instrument flight, and the pilot had to have an instrument rating issued by the government. Military aircraft came under the same regulations, with the agreement of the armed forces, so that theoretically there would be no airplane in the sky in instrument weather not equipped to fly in these conditions and no pilot not qualified to do the flying.

Instrument flight also required the pilot to file a flight plan if visibility was less than one mile. Flight plans had to be approved and accepted by air traffic control authorities. Aircraft flying on instruments along a civil airway were separated by the rules both horizontally and vertically: planes flying east were required to fly at odd-thousand-foot altitudes, westbound aircraft at even thousands of feet. Deviation was permitted only in an emergency, on orders from or with permission of ATC, or when crossing an airway intersection, when the airplane was required to climb 500 feet above its normal cruising altitude.

Since there were now two systems of control working hand-in-hand—one at the airport, one along the airways—aircraft were,

Jimmy Doolittle, a test pilot at the Air Corps' Wright Field (Ohio) Research Center, demonstrated the first instrument landings and takeoffs in 1929.

in theory, covered all along their route of flight, from takeoff to landing, and the improvement in morale, both among the flying community and the general public, was marked. The control procedure began with the filing of a flight plan with the airline's dispatching office, which immediately passed it on to flight control. It was up to the controller to assign a takeoff time and cruising altitude and to approve the route or suggest changes because of traffic or weather. From then until he arrived at his destination, the pilot was required to issue regular reports every time he passed over a designated radio fix, and in this manner accurate track could be kept of his progress along the route. Conflicting traffic could be avoided by radioing instructions of change course or altitude.

The biggest headache came, not surprisingly, at the airport of arrival. All incoming aircraft were required to pass over a radio beacon, just outside the airport perimeter, called the inner marker. Three or more aircraft arriving simultaneously at the inner marker were enough to constitute dangerous congestion. They had to be separated by altitude and, in some cases, asked to circle at a given altitude until the runway was clear. Pilots and airlines naturally detested these "holding patterns," which could delay arrival by a half-hour or more, but it was the only way in which a safe and orderly procedure of bringing aircraft down to the runway could be guaranteed.

As mentioned previously, Newark, Chicago, and Cleveland were the first three airports to try out this new system of airways and airport traffic control. They were, of course, only the tip of the iceberg as far as the air traffic problem was concerned, and once it was obvious that the new system worked, there was pressure to get it installed elsewhere. Washington, D.C., Los Angeles, the San Francisco-Oakland area, Detroit, and Pittsburgh were next on the list, and such was the pressure that the Department of Commerce promised that these cities, too, would have Air Traffic Control organizations set up and working before the coming winter.

However, it turned out that ATC was itself only the tip of the iceberg as far as the massive problems of aviation in the United States were concerned. The Detroit system became operational more or less on schedule, and Pittsburgh was under ATC not long after. But from then on the story turns horrendous: it was as though, having finally developed and introduced a system to bring some order into the chaos of laissez-faire flying as the United States had practiced it since the Wright brothers' times, the system itself now acted as a mirror of just how complex and enormous the job really was.

Chapter 5
ATC on the Cheap

It was the winter of 1936-37, and to some Americans it seemed as though the sky were falling in. On December 15 a Western Air Express flight inexplicably disappeared between Los Angeles and Salt Lake City. Another Western Air Express flight crashed three weeks later; by that time there had been five fatal air crashes, with 32 people killed. Beyond atrocious weather, there seemed to be no ready explanation for this rash of disasters, but coming as it did just as the Bureau of Air Commerce was introducing its new system of air traffic control, it made the heat for more and better air safety measures almost unbearable.

There was no problem with money this time, as there had been in the austerity days of the first Roosevelt administration. Even the president, inexplicably slow as he had sometimes proved to be in the past on matters of aviation policy, had no hesitations about the urgency this time. The problem was far more difficult to resolve than that. The basic cause was an acute shortage of manpower.

How does one go about drumming up a body of men for an exacting job that has never existed before? There were experienced men in airport control towers, but all of these were already working for Air Traffic Control (ATC). And, in any case, the airport tower jobs were not as demanding or as urgent as those of the airways controllers. Finally, once they had been hired and trained, all the controllers had to be taught how to mesh so closely that no airplane flying through American skies could slip through the ATC net and cause trouble.

The entrance requirements were stringent enough to bar a good many would-be applicants. A high school diploma was required, to which was coupled a four-hour examination. In addition, an applicant was required to have either 1,000 hours of flying experience or one year's experience in an airline's operations office or experience in controlling airplane traffic.

Nor could the evident rigors of the job be offset by attractive salaries. The layman's expectations were for salaries somewhere in the $6,000 to $8,000 range, and some even expected that the job would bring with it a private airplane. The reality was that a station manager earned $3,500 a year, an assistant managed $2,900, and controllers could expect $2,000.

Finding personnel was not the only problem, either; it turned out that many pilots had to be educated to fly under such strict control from the ground. Pilots were still free and easy, going back into the cabin to converse with passengers and keep them at ease. If they missed a checkpoint here or there along a familiar route, it did not seem to make much difference to them. On the ground, however, such carelessness was enough to make a controller distraught: where was Flight so-and-so which should have reported over Lake Thus-and-Such 15 minutes ago? Once there was a hole in the orderly parade of airplanes proceeding through the skies toward their destination, nobody could say with any certainty what was really happening.

Worst of all was the holding pattern delay, which was almost inevitable at certain airports and at certain times of day. In one case, a pilot at Newark, held up for more than 45 minutes on a particularly crowded afternoon, simply made up his mind that he was going to land without permission and forthwith proceeded to do so. Traffic control rather than the traffic itself took the brunt of the blame for the irritating, empty minutes spent swinging around a holding point while other aircraft landed and discharged their passengers. Some airlines even announced "arrivals delayed by traffic control" without explaining to the passengers why the delay was necessary.

It was around this time that pilots of general aviation—all forms of aviation outside of the scheduled carriers and the military—and private pilots first began their continuing complaints about being "legislated out of the skies." One can only imagine what the volume of the outcry would have been had Eugene Vidal's grandiose project for a "flivver" plane gone through. It was also the

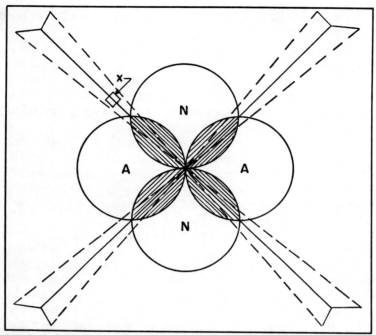

America's first airway radio system broadcast a low frequency beam in four directions, with a Morse Code *N* defining one edge of the beam and an *A* the other edge. When homing on the signal centerline, the *A* and *N* blended to give the pilot a steady tone in his earphones—provided that static from storms did not render the signal largely ineffective. This system was in use from the thirties to well into the fifties.

time when the first suggestions were made that private aircraft without certain specified items of equipment—two-way radio, for example—simply be barred from landing at large terminals. Vidal publicly announced that such measures were being considered, but they never actually came to pass.

What did take place was a spreading realization that air traffic control alone could not solve commercial aviation's growing safety problems. Those who knew most about it—men like Eugene Vidal, Senator Royal S. Copeland, and J. Carroll Cone, Vidal's executive assistant—knew what it was: some sense and order had to be brought into the vast, amorphous, and largely uncataloged mass of aviation regulations that had accumulated over the years of mismanagement. A new supervisory body—independent and with real teeth—had to be created to make air traffic control a truly effective, working reality.

When it came, Eugene Vidal departed. He had shepherded the

Bureau of Air Commerce through frustrating, stormy, money-starved years, and he was not sorry to leave. More and more the sentiment in both the government and the private sector was that all authority for aviation matters should rest in the hands of a single federal body. And this is the way it finally was established: there was a completely reorganized Bureau of Air Commerce, and this time it was given a broom that could sweep clean.

Some of its problems might have seemed laughable had they not been so fraught with potential tragedy. In Washington, D.C., the nation's capital, the traffic control station was in a room measuring 125 square feet. In this cubicle five men, crammed in with two Teletype machines, a map table, a filing cabinet, a desk, and the boards on which aircraft progress through the skies outside was registered had to see to the safe arrival of airplanes carrying the nation's legislators, diplomats, businessmen—and they had to have this place manned 24 hours a day. When they were finally moved into larger temporary quarters, the roof leaked, the floor was warped, and not a door could be opened or shut without kicking, hauling, and swearing.

Working conditions at virtually every station were abominable. Controllers were in such short supply that they could not be given vacations and in many cases could not even get weekends off. They worked 10 to 12 hours a day as a matter of course, although nominally they were on a 44-hour week. They routinely showed signs of dangerous fatigue and irritability, a potentially fatal flaw when dealing with a pilot in trouble.

Now came the question of the Bureau of Air Commerce—hitherto responsible for managing traffic on the airways—taking over the airport towers as well. Here, too, it is hard not to laugh at what was in store for the bureau. A complaint from the Detroit airway station manager detailed what was going on at the Wayne County Airport Control Tower along his route. "The tower operators are required, while on duty in the tower, to act as telephone switchboard operators handling all airport incoming and outgoing calls." This was by no means unusual. Control towers were built, paid for, and maintained with local funds, and they had to exist as best they could within local budgets. If there wasn't enough money for telephone operators, then controllers would have to do the job.

Since taking over the towers was out of the question at this time, the bureau tried to standardize the expertise of control tower operators by insisting that they be federally licensed. Here, too, there was trouble—states' rights kind of trouble. It is amazing to read almost half a century later how many other priorities officials managed to get in before acknowledging the one overriding priority of all—that of saving lives in airplanes. But the bureau found a way to force this much at least in the interest of safety by using the air traffic rules that made federal licenses mandatory for pilots in instrument weather to cover use of federally licensed control tower operators as well.

There were at that time 53 "control airports" serving air carriers in the country and in at least one of them, Akron, Ohio, controllers not only had to handle airplane traffic but also sell tickets, answer the telephone, and handle the passengers' baggage. Nonetheless, by fits and starts, the system was moving in the right direction, and the new era in aviation, however haltingly, was slowly getting under way.

The new era was to be quite different from the old one in many other respects. The Years of the Passenger were about to begin, and the consequences would be far-reaching. Unobserved by the general public, the financial basis of flying had shifted away from the airmail subsidies, which fell victim to unseemly squabbles between the Post Office and the Interstate Commerce Commission, to a vendetta by the Roosevelt administration against the airlines for their part in building the system under Walter Folger Brown. As a consequence, airlines lost money hand over fist in the years from 1934 to 1936, and they had to look to the passenger, that hitherto neglected adjunct to the bulging airmail sacks, to keep them alive. And by a stroke of good fortune, an airplane was at hand to save them just when they needed it most.

We mentioned the Douglas DC-3, "the world's most beloved transport plane," earlier. By 1936 this versatile aircraft could carry 21 passengers between New York and California in 16 hours, at an operating cost 50 percent lower than the Boeing B-247D (an improved version of the original B-247), its nearest competitor. It was the first airplane in history that could make money just by carrying passengers, and this fact revolutionized the air transport industry.

On the other hand, it also carried the seeds of destruction within itself. The old airmail routes had been protected against intrusion by unsanctioned competitors; passenger routes were not. Anybody wanting to get into business with a passenger route could do so and thereby possibly put a long-established competitor, with a heavy investment in his line, out of business. Within the aviation industry voices once again began calling out for government regulation to put some order into the threatening chaos of passenger traffic and to give established operators the protection they needed.

It was a long time coming, but in 1938 it came at last in the form of a single organization, partly the child of the Congress, partly the creature of the president, which incorporated all matters pertaining to civil aviation. The public, long indifferent to the economic welfare of the airlines which were of such urgent concern to businessmen, Congress, and the administration, had finally recognized the much broader base of the aviation regulation issue—the issue of safety in the air.

The name of the organization was the Civil Aeronautics Authority (CAA), changed by amendment in 1940 to the Civil Aeronau-

Juan Trippe (left) and Charles Lindbergh. From a small beginning in the late twenties, Trippe built Pan American World Airways into the world's largest overseas air carrier.

tics Administration, and its effect was the recognition that civil air transport had come of age in the United States. The states' rights issue had been argued out of existence: it was now generally recognized that matters such as aircraft licensing and inspection, aircraft route control, pilots' licensing, and all other aspects of these machines that overflew states' boundaries with such majestic hauteur could only sensibly be dealt with by the federal government. At the top of such a regulating body there needed to be one man who would administer the whole. In years to come, some extremely able men would fill that job.

It was high time. In 1938, the year the Civil Aeronautics Act became law, U.S. airlines flew 69.7 million revenue miles and carried 1.3 million passengers. In the 12 years since the enactment of the Air Commerce Act, which first recognized that civil aviation existed in the United States, America had become the leading civil air power of the world. Regular transoceanic flights with passengers were only a year away. And only three years away lay Pearl Harbor and the Great War, when American air power would spread around the world.

Chapter 6
VHF—A Giant Step

To read the mandate of the Federal Aviation Administration (FAA) is to realize with something close to awe the immense power this agency wields over anything that has to do with flying in American skies. Born in 1938 out of the Air Commerce Act of 1926, the FAA supplanted the Civil Aeronautics Board (CAB) in 1958 as the regulatory agency for all nonmilitary aviation in the United States. In 1967 it became a part of the Department of Transportation. Today its responsibilities include the regulation of air commerce to foster aviation safety, promote civil aviation, and establish a national system of airports; it must also ensure the most efficient use of navigable airspace and foster the development and operation of a common system of air traffic control and air navigation for both civilian and military aircraft.

The FAA issues and enforces rules, regulations, and minimum standards relating to the manufacture, operation, and maintenance of aircraft, as well as the rating and certification (including medical) of airmen and the certification of airports serving air carriers that have been certified by the Civil Aeronautics Board. It also performs flight inspection of air navigation facilities in the United States and, as required, abroad.

The FAA provides a system for the registration of an aircraft's nationality, its engines, propellers, and appliances as well as a system for recording aircraft ownership.

Today, general aviation is many things. More than 40 percent of all new light-planes are purchased for business use.

It is also responsible for research and development activities serving the establishment and for the maintenance of a safe and efficient system of air navigation and air traffic control to meet the needs of both civil aviation and the air defense system. The agency is also involved in developing and testing improved aircraft, engines, propellers, and appliances.

In the field of air navigation, the FAA is responsible for the location, construction, maintenance, and operation of federal visual and electronic aids to air navigation. It operates and maintains communications equipment, radio teletype circuits and equipment, and equipment at air traffic control towers and centers.

To ensure safe and efficient use of navigable airspace, the FAA operates a network of airport control towers, air route traffic control centers, and flight service stations. It develops air traffic rules and regulations and allocates the use of the airspace. It also provides for the security control of air traffic to meet national defense requirements.

Perhaps most surprising is the FAA's involvement with civil aviation abroad. Under the Federal Aviation Act and the International Aviation Facilities Act of 1948, the agency is charged with promoting civil aviation abroad by the assignment of technical groups, the training of foreign nations, and the exchange of information with foreign governments. It provides technical representation at international conferences, including participation in the International Civil Aviation Organization and other international organizations.

With respect to airports, the FAA administers programs to identify the type and cost of development of public airports required

General aviation is also agricultural flying. Aerial pest-control greatly increases food production in the United States.

Private aircraft place key people quickly on the scene to make critical decisions at countless spots not served by the airlines. (Courtesy, Beech Aircraft Corporation)

for a national airport system and to provide grants of funds to assist public agencies in airport system planning, airport master planning, and public airport development.

As if all this weren't enough, the FAA also administers the aviation insurance and aircraft load guarantee programs. It is an allotting agency under the Defense Materials System with respect to priorities and allocation for civil aircraft and civil aviation operations. The FAA also develops specifications for the preparation of aeronautical charts. It publishes current information on airways and airport service and issues technical publications for the improvement of safety in flight, airport planning and design, and other aeronautical activities.

To administer its huge empire, the FAA has divided the continental United States into ten regions, and the rest of the world into two more: Pacific-Asia, with headquarters in Honolulu; and Europe and Africa/Middle East, with headquarters in Brussels. There are, in addition to these major field organizations, the Mike Monroney Aeronautical Center in Oklahoma City; the FAA Technical Center in Atlantic City, where such new equipment as the automatic landing system is developed and tested; and the Metropolitan Washington Airports office, with headquarters at National Airport.

If there is anything the FAA has overlooked in its amassing to itself of everything pertaining to aviation in the United States, it would surely take an experienced nitpicker equipped with a microscope to find it. But the good news is that the building of this empire need offend no one, although in truth it offends many. That there are things wrong with the FAA, that there are areas in which it is deficient, need surprise no one, and we shall deal with these matters in due course. Meanwhile it is only fair to report that civil aviation is administered in the United States is the safest in the world and that the FAA really does take its responsibility for passenger safety extremely seriously. A look behind the scenes at how aviation functions in this country under the benevolent despotism of the FAA will also show why aviators as taxpayers tend to rejoice: here is one area in which they get their money's worth for what they pay to Uncle Sam.

Most passengers believe that American airspace is pretty much what they see out of the window when they are aloft. There is the immensity of vaulting sky, usually a deep, clear blue at the cruising altitude of modern jets. There, far below, may be a floor of clouds hiding the earth across which the plane is traveling at a speed of around 500 miles per hour. Once in a great while the passenger may see another airplane, above or below his own, or he may spot, far above, the contrails of another jet. But mainly the sky seems empty and trackless, a huge void that the airplane navigates in some fashion which, to the layman back there in the passenger compartment, can only seem mysterious and a little bit miraculous.

But now consider how the airspace—which is the same as the sky—looks to the FAA and, through the FAA, to the pilot and crew flying the airplane. To do this we have only to take one of the many Area Charts or En Route Charts, which the FAA publishes and which are available to any pilot. These charts are not maps in the conventional sense of the word; they do not show the land except as a vaguely indicated outline along the shore. These are true maps of the sky, and what they show is a bewildering maze of the highways the FAA has spun between its electronic navigation guides, the modern radio beacons.

These are identified on the chart as very-high-frequency omniranges or VORs. Many pilots know them simply as Omnis. The term indicates their most outstanding feature: a VOR beacon sends out 359 straight-line signals that radiate like the spokes of a wheel from the center of a compass rose. Thus there is a signal—or radial, to use the airman's terminology—for every degree on the compass.

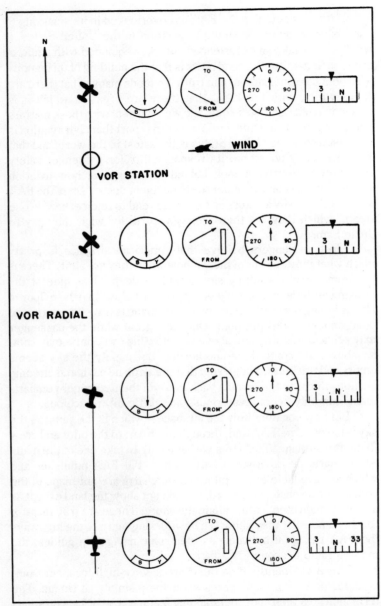

Today's VOR air navigation system is made up of more than 400 very high frequency transmitters that broadcast signals in all directions, allowing pilots to accurately navigate anywhere in the country. This illustration depicts how the VOR system compensates for wind when the pilot keeps the needle centered.

The beacon itself can be identified by the frequency on which it transmits, which is indicated on the pilot's chart. The radial that the pilot wants to use can be picked up by turning the Omni Bearing Selector. Let us say, for example, that the pilot, having identified his approximate position somewhere within range of the beacon, now wishes to fly to the beacon and shape his course from there. He will first tune in on the beacon's frequency and will hear its call letters transmitted in code and, in many cases, hear a voice identification as well. Next, he will turn his Omni Bearing Selector until the needle on the dial moves toward the center. At the same time the word *TO* will appear in a small window on the dial.

Let us say that the pilot finds his Omni Bearing Selector is turned to 095. This means that the radial he has picked up corresponds to 095 degrees on the compass rose, or almost due east. He has now established with certainty the direction in which he is flying and can set his gyrocompass by it. He can, if he wishes, find his exact position either by taking a cross-bearing on another VOR beacon or by intercepting another airway. In any event, sooner or later he will reach the beacon toward which he is flying. As he crosses over it,

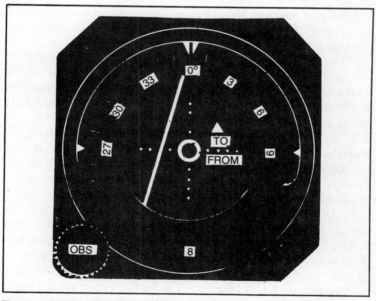

The use of the VOR requires that the pilot set his bearing selector knob (lower left) according to his desired course and tune his radio to the proper station. The needle indicates any deviation from his heading, and the *TO-FROM* indicator tells him which quadrant of the selected beam he is flying.

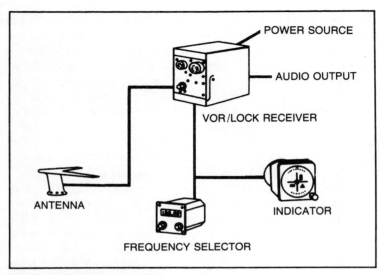

A typical VOR receiver installation.

the indicator on his instrument dial will change from *TO* to *FROM* and, for good measure, the needle will swing widely before centering again. Thus the pilot will know exactly where he is: right above the beacon.

The FAA, as we have seen, is responsible for the installation and maintenance of the radio beacon system; it is also responsible for the network of aerial highways, or airways, that crisscrosses the sky from one corner of the country to the other. These are generally set up to correspond to a certain radial and, somewhere around halfway, will intersect with another radial from the next VOR beacon down the line. The pilot, therefore, can work his way through the sky to his destination much as if he were flying along a highway in the sky, except that, rather than a yellow center line, his Omni receiver is the controlling factor in guiding him on his way.

Nor is this all. The pilot en route along the airways is never alone. He is in constant communication with the ground—with ground controllers at airports he is overflying and with the Flight Service Stations along his route. The latter are the pilot's greatest friends. They will give him weather information, Airport Advisory Service with pertinent information about the airport toward which he is heading; they will aid him with emergency information for in-flight crises. This is particularly helpful if a pilot gets lost or becomes disoriented. The Flight Service Station can bring not only radar to bear on the problem but also local information about conspicuous landmarks that can help the pilot locate himself.

The VOR beacons also do double duty by functioning as weather information stations. Those with voice facilities will broadcast the latest weather advisories at 15 minutes past the hour. If hazardous conditions prevail, they will also broadcast these at more frequent intervals in the form of AIRMETS (news of weather potentially hazardous to pilots of limited experience or aircraft with limited equipment) and SIGMETS (conditions potentially hazardous to *all* aircraft in flight). This type of weather advisory can indicate anything from severe thunderstorms to tornadoes, and it is safe to say that any pilot will give them due heed.

Airplanes traveling long distances, such as airliners, are constantly monitored in flight by the FAA's Air Route Traffic Control Centers (ARTCC). As they progress along their route they will traverse the territory monitored by such an ARTCC and will then be "handed off" to the next one until they arrive at their destination and are handed off to the tower at the airport to which they are bound.

There are 20 such ARTCCs covering major airways in the United States. One such—or rather a facility exercising such a function in a particularly congested area—is the New York Terminal Radar Approach Control or TRACON as it is known. TRACON is responsible for all of the aircraft approaching or departing from the metropolitan airports in New York, which are among the busiest

Many modern business aircraft are as well instrumented as airliners and with air transport-rated pilots in command, fully utilize the ATC system.

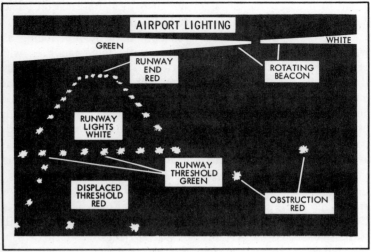

Airport lighting, too, keeps pace with the Jet Age.

in the world. It covers an area extending up to 80 miles around Kennedy, La Guardia, and Newark airports.

TRACON has been in existence since 1968. Until that year, each of the three airports had handled its own traffic independently of the others, using medium-range radar to control incoming and outgoing aircraft. By 1968, however, it was obvious that this way of doing things was no longer adequate to handle the combined traffic of three airports safely. As a temporary measure pending a permanent solution, the medium-range radars were removed from the control towers and installed in one common place, the Common Instrument Flight Room in Hangar 11 at Kennedy Airport. Here the controllers worked together to coordinate the flow of traffic into the three airports.

It took TRACON more than a decade to get organized into its present form. When it did it was a model of the most modern, automated, computerized facility available—a showcase of how the FAA sees the future. A visit there today conveys a vivid impression not only of disciplined handling of what is essentially a chaotic problem but also of an environment that is mindful of science fiction as seen by Hollywood.

The heart and center of the facility in Garden City, Long Island, is an enormous, shadowy room in which dim figures move about on hushed feet and tiny red, green, and blue lights wink constantly like fireflies. There are no windows, and the light is so subdued as to

In case of complete radio failure aboard an aircraft, the tower has a light-signal gun handy to provide essential directions to aircraft within the control area.

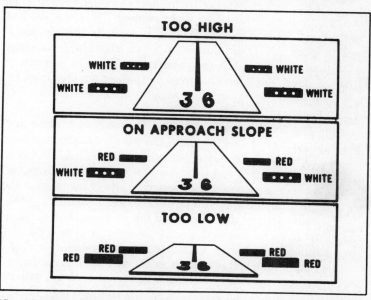

Visual Approach Slope Indicator (VASI) is a light system that provides pilots with visual reference for a proper landing approach.

appear hazy. It is impossible to tell how many people are at work here, but there are some 300 controllers, supervisors, and administrative air traffic personnel working around-the-clock in eight-hour shifts, so one might guess that there are close to a hundred.

Once the eyes have grown accustomed to the dim light, the radar sets become visible: 44 round, 21-inch screens with a pencil-line of brilliant green light circling endlessly on the screen, lighting up the blips that mark each aircraft, the data blocks that accompany them, and the other information displayed. With these 44 radars, the TRACON facility has a theoretical capability of handling 1,200 aircraft at a time—five times as many as could be handled from the hangar room at Kennedy Airport.

In this dim room the modern miracle of communication between an airplane and the ground is displayed. Each airplane comes to TRACON from the New York Air Route Traffic Control Centers (ARTCC) which monitor the final phase of the airliners' en route flights. The TRACON controller takes the "handoff" from ARTCC and identifies the airplane from the blip and the data block on his radar screen. From then on he is responsible for guiding this airplane down through the Terminal Control Area (TCA) and onto the proper runway.

The data block gives him all of the necessary information about the airplane: it identifies it by flight number ("Eastern 505") or registration ("Piper Nan-9013-Delta"); it gives its altitude, and it gives its speed. All of this information comes from a huge computer on the floor directly below the radar room. There is no radar at TRACON itself; the information comes to the computer from remote radar installations, and the computer then transcribes it into the information on the data blocks.

Pilot and controller are, of course, in steady communication, and one of the first things the controller asks for is the airplane's altitude. This is done so that a comparison may be made between what the computer says and what the pilot reads off his altimeter. Altitude, of course, is one of the most vital bits of information the controller has, and he wants to be sure he has it right.

The radar screen, then, has all of the information needed for safety: aircraft identity, speed, altitude, and course. The controller is in a position to see how his airplane stands in relation to all the others on the screen and to steer it safely past hazards on its way down to the runway. And he has the computer as back-up, with its ability to flash a "conflict alert" if it sees a collision impending.

The electronic equipment at TRACON is known in its entirety

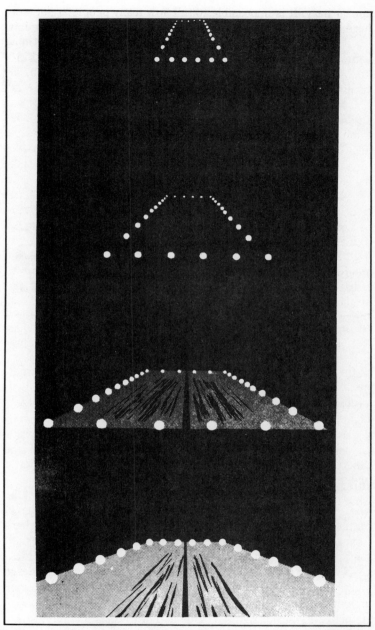

A night-landing approach depicting the effectiveness of the aircraft's landing lights (top to bottom) as touchdown nears.

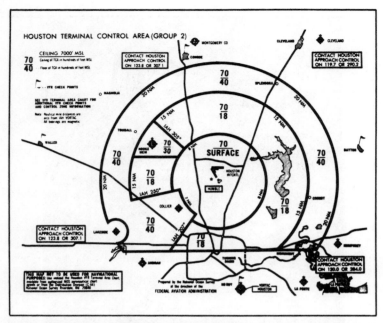

Houston Terminal Control Area. The bold numbers, one above the other, indicate ceiling and floor of the TCA in hundreds of feet.

as the Automated Radar Terminal System (ARTS). It is the largest installation of its type in the United States, and it requires a highly skilled technical staff working 24 hours a day to maintain it at its highest level of reliability. The technicians involved take a 30-week course of formal classroom instruction at the FAA Academy in Oklahoma City, Oklahoma. The formal training provides a basis of theoretical knowledge to which is then added practical experience under a crew chief or senior technicians.

Controllers, too, must go through their period of training at the FAA Academy. They are required to attend an 18-week course of formal classroom training, after which they will spend anywhere from two to four years working their way up at an FAA facility until they become Full Performance Level (FPL) controllers. At TRACON only FPL controllers are accepted, and these must undergo additional intensive training for a full year. The training program includes not only on-the-job instruction but also practice on simulators, which can project any kind of traffic situation desired, from normal takeoffs or landings to sudden emergencies and imminent crashes.

The terminal radars are the keys to the uninterrupted operations at the busy hub airports.

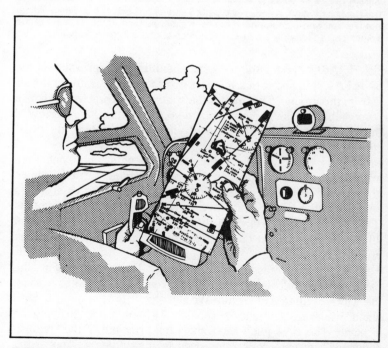

Flying cross-country, the pilot relying on radio navigation aids also checks his progress on the appropriate chart, while Air Route Traffic Control, observing his transponder signature on radar is aware of his position and track.

The Cessna Citation business jet ("bizjet") serves corporations as a mini-airliner that flies anywhere as the need arises. Neither surface transportation nor the airlines can adequately serve the travel needs of the larger companies.

TRACON is, for the moment, the ultimate expression of the basic FAA philosophy that the best way to regulate traffic in the air is from the ground. This makes the controller, in practice, the man responsible for safety since he is the one who has the overview of the total traffic situation around an airport through his radar screens.

There are powerful arguments for this philosophy, but there are also powerful reasons for dissent. A running battle has been going on for years between the FAA and the dissenters, chief among whom are the pilots of "general aviation"—the noncommercial fliers of corporation jets and business aircraft, "flying doctors," and "flying farmers," right on down to student pilots doing their first cross-country solos.

What are the reasons for this dissent? There is, first of all, the basic aviation philosophy, going back through Charles Lindbergh all the way to Wilbur and Orville Wright, that it is "the pilot in command" who has the ultimate responsibility for decisions in flying the airplane. The FAA itself recognizes the principle of the "pilot in command" by numerous references to his or her person in the Federal Aviation Regulations (FARs). In paragraph 91.3 of FAR the principle is defined: "The pilot in command of an aircraft is directly

directly responsible for, and is the final authority as to, the operation of that aircraft." He is, in short, the man who sits in the left seat, the traditional seat of command, the man who flies the airplane.

This is a very strong tradition with most pilots, for, as pointed out earlier in this book, one of the first things a beginning pilot learns is how final his responsibility is when he flies an airplane. It is not like driving a car, steering a boat, or operating the locomotive of a train. There is no room to forgive a wrong decision, no way to retract a wrong move, nothing that can give a pilot under stress a moment of respite to think his situation over and resolve it in a peaceful and reasoned way.

Pilots are trained to think in these terms, to accept the awful responsibility that they have and do their job in full awareness of it. What, then, must it be like for a pilot to turn over his authority to a

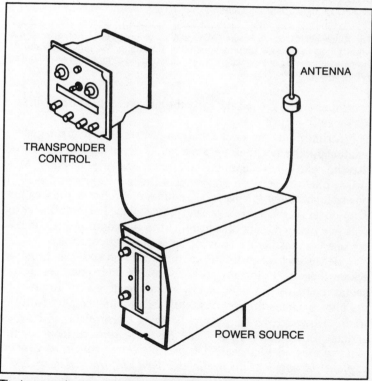

ANTENNA

TRANSPONDER
CONTROL

POWER SOURCE

The transponder may "squawk" an almost infinite number of codes selected by the pilot that, when interrogated by an air traffic controller, positively identify the aircraft on the controller's radar screen. Coupled with an encoding altimeter, the transponder will also report the plane's altitude.

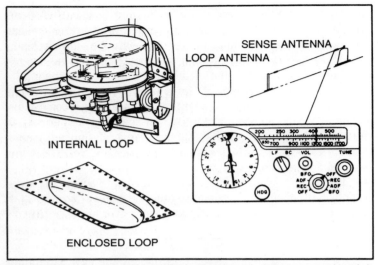

The Automatic Direction Finder (ADF) is a simple low-frequency receiver that, when tuned to any LF ground transmitter (including AM radio stations) will indicate the bearing of the station tuned relative to the aircraft. It is an old but still very useful air navigation aid.

controller on the ground and to fly the airplane only as this man says he should?

Airline pilots can handle this somewhat better than can general aviation pilots since their very method of flying already recognizes that the controllers must be given part of the responsibility. Most airline pilots fly on IFR (instrument flight rules) instead of VFR (visual flight rules) as a matter of routine, regardless of the weather. They do this in the interest of safety, since they thereby transfer the "see and be seen" rule of visual flight to the controller. He is now the one responsible for spotting an impending collision.

Because of this attitude, the pilot may go so far as to fail to acknowledge a "traffic advisory" from a ground controller. If this seems foolhardy, consider that by acknowledging a traffic advisory the pilot assumes the responsibility for avoiding conflict with the traffic. However, as busy as he is flying the airplane on its pre-scribed course, he may well not have the time to look out the window and find the threatening aircraft. Worse still, *he may see an airplane, identify it as his traffic, and then keep track of it, unaware that it is the wrong airplane!* This may be what happened in a San Diego crash in 1978 that killed 144 people.

Thus, in order to cope with what they believe to be some of the more unreasonable aspects of the FAA rules and with what the ground controllers tell them to do, pilots have made up some private rules of their own. Needless to say, this is not a healthy situation and everyone recognizes this; but until something better comes along it will have to do.

Another reason for dissent with the FAA lies primarily with the pilots of general aviation. This is the increasing cost of the equipment required by the FAA to fly in Terminal Control Areas (TCAs). The principal bone of contention here is the transponder, that marvelous instrument that automatically transmits the airplane's altitude and speed along with its identification. A transponder may cost from $5,000 up, and to add this amount to an airplane that already has several thousand dollars worth of electronic gear aboard may well be too much for the private pilot.

Meanwhile TRACON exists perhaps as a symbol of the closest one can get to perfection in an imperfect world. As one of the staff joyously shouted on the afternoon of the day the new $25 million facility was commissioned, when it had brought its first airplane safely down onto the runway at Kennedy Airport: "Hey, fellows! *It works!*"

Chapter 7
Separation

In July, 1955, an event took place in Seattle, Washington that, might with considerable justification be called the "Second Coming of the Airplane." On July 15, Boeing conducted the first, and entirely successful, test flight of the 707, the first American jet transport. The Jet Age had begun.

The jet transport did more than revolutionize commercial flying. It virtually changed it from the ground up. The Boeing 707 could carry more passengers than its piston-powered counterparts, and above all it could carry them at more than twice the speed. New York-Paris now became a matter of seven hours or less flying time; New York-Los Angeles, about five. There was a quantum jump in comfort, too, since jets flew at extremely high altitudes—40,000 feet being by no means unusual—in order to maximize fuel economy. Weather was scarcely a factor any more. The jets might have to fly through clouds, rain, or snow to reach their cruising altitude, but most of the time they were well above the weather. And the jet engine was by far the most reliable power plant aviation had ever had, a fact that was a boon to management, pilots, and crew.

But along with its advantages, the jet also brought a host of problems, and the Civil Aeronautics Administration (CAA), the federal regulatory agency, was prepared for virtually none of them. Austerity had cut its ranks so thin that the Civil Aeronautics Board's Airworthiness Division, responsible for supervising design requirements for all types of new aircraft, had only four technicians and three secretaries to cope with a totally new and different type of aircraft. And the rest of the regulatory apparatus was in a more or less similar state of unreadiness to handle the stream of problems that the 707 brought in its wake.

These were numerous and pervasive. How long a runway would be required for regular commercial jet traffic? How much load would runways routinely have to bear? How could jets best cope with bad weather and high-velocity gusts? After all, they would have to fly through poor weather on their landing approaches. What sorts of problems would be posed by cabin pressurization at altitudes of 40,000 feet or more? What about noise on the ground, or close to the ground? And how could collisions be avoided between aircraft that would be approaching each other at closure speeds of more than 1,000 miles per hour?

Some of the jet's problems had been pioneered by the British, who already had the deHavilland Comet in operation. But the Comet, at first a triumph, had run into trouble. A rash of inexplicable crashes had forced the grounding of the plane while extensive—and expensive—tests were undertaken for structural fatigue. American manufacturers had been able to benefit from these tests, beefing up their airframes and, in particular, strengthening areas that the British tests had revealed as weak. But there was a detrimental side to this as well. In the absence of any American jets, some airlines were beginning to buy the British products, notably the British Viscount turboprop, an airplane that combined a jet power plant with a propeller drive. Not as fast as a jet, it was nonetheless faster and cheaper to operate than a piston-powered airplane.

But the presence of the jet could not be denied. By the spring of 1956, all the arguments had been argued and the decision had come down squarely in favor of the new planes: one billion dollars worth of them had been ordered by the airlines. It would be another two years before the planes could be built and certificated, which was precious little time to get ready for them. For there was no doubt any longer that they were coming.

The CAA used the time well. Aware that it was operating on a system that was already outdated for piston-engine craft, agency safety experts looked on the jet as a problem airplane rather than as the blessing it obviously seemed to the flying public. As a first step, the Civil Aeronautics Administration compiled a list of "100 Jet Age Problems." Anything and everything that anybody could think of went onto that list, from cockpit visibility and the problem of

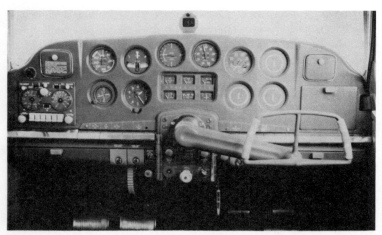

The instrument panel of the 1947 Beechcraft Bonanza featured a single transceiver for VOR tracking and voice communications.

1,000-plus mile-per-hour closure speeds to the possible use of drag parachutes to shorten landing runs. Even medical problems were considered: how would continuous high altitude and high speed flight affect crew members?

Airports, of course, were a major problem: they were geared to handle airplanes with 80 passengers embarking or disembarking. Now they would be getting them 150 or more at a clip. Did this mean more congestion, more delays at departure gates? What about handling the baggage of such crowds?

Noise was another irksome problem, but here the CAA could turn to the Air Force which had already been flying jets for some years. In 1956 the Air Force sponsored a Jet Age Conference and suggested there were three ways of handling the noise factor: one, "sell" it through a public relations campaign pointing out that noise was a small price to pay for this kind of technological progress; two, "diminish" it by somehow muffling it; and three, "move" it by instituting landing and takeoff procedures that would take aircraft away from densely populated areas. Option one was never even considered; two was at last worked out to a certain degree, although no jet engine can ever be muffled in the true sense of the word; and three, to the alarm and disgust of pilots, was finally adopted in places where the noise problem was really crucial, as at New York's Idlewild (now Kennedy) Airport. The takeoff patterns were altered in such a way that departing jets made turns away from populated areas as soon as it was deemed safe to do so, thus adding a new hazard for pilots to worry about as they started training to fly the new airplanes.

The "100 Jet Age Problems" were an imaginative and intelligent beginning, but the CAA was well aware that this was only the start of its problems. The agency in its present form had been in existence since 1938; it had survived the war and spread the doctrine of effective air traffic control more widely than it had ever been spread before. But now, going on 20 years after the massive reorganization that had created it, it was once again shopworn, short of funds, short of personnel, and short of modern equipment. Congressmen flew happily around the country on commercial airliners that were still, in many cases, dependent on navigation aids and procedures that were about as up-to-date as the lighthouse, but they seemed strangely unaware of this when funds for modernizing the CAA came up for discussion in the House or Senate. They couldn't even decide on what to do about their own airport at Washington, D.C., which was probably the most antiquated major airport in the country and so dangerously overburdened that it was officially described as "supersaturated." One congressman, reaching for the strongest rhetoric he could find, put it thus:

"Sooner or later, God forbid, something tragic is going to happen at the Washington National Airport. Everybody around this

The instrument panel of a 1981 Beechcraft Bonanza reflects the continuing "electronic revolution" in air navigation. The avionics (aviation electronics) in this panel would have paid for two complete Bonanzas in 1947.

An unanticipated threat to air safety appeared in the early sixties, and Attorney General Robert Kennedy ordered this notice posted in all public airports.

table knows what is going on over there or what may happen . . . . The place is saturated with air traffic. We are being saved by technicians and mechanical contrivances. We need another airport, now—last night was too late."

The problem of Washington National was symptomatic, really, of the continuing problem of American air transport as a whole. In early 1956—which, don't forget, was an election year—the troubles on the airways and at the airports received another dramatic boost in the form of the long-awaited Harding Report, commissioned by President Dwight Eisenhower to conduct a thorough review of

American aviation policy, its existing situation and its needs. Headed by William Barclay Harding and studded with men who, like himself, had actual aviation experience, the Harding Aviation Facilities Study Group had taken its mandate seriously, and its recommendations were certain to carry weight.

Those who were concerned about air safety were not disappointed. "Much of our airspace is already overcrowded," the report said. "The development of airports, navigation aids, and especially our air traffic control system is lagging far behind both aeronautical development and the needs of our mobile population and of our industry . . . . Risks of midair collisions have already reached critical proportions, and . . . the collision hazard is becoming greater as the increases in civil and military air traffic outpace the capabilities of outmoded traffic control facilities."

There was more, much more, and the conclusion of the whole report was a strong recommendation for a thoroughgoing review leading to a national Aviation Facilities program. The Harding Report felt that the study should be undertaken by the executive branch and that the nation's aviation program should be directed by one man serving "under a temporary appointment in the Executive Office of the president."

This report came in the nick of time. If it needed any confirmation by events, it got it in June when the worst traffic jam anyone could remember tied up the nation's airways in a manner reminiscent of the Los Angeles freeways at rush hour. New York was blocked for 14 hours, Washington for 12, and 30,000 passengers had to cancel their travel plans. It took days for air travel to get back to normal again. Four days later Najeeb Halaby, himself a pilot and Harding's vice-chairman on the committee, described the situation to a congressional committee:

"You must understand what the United States is up against [and] recognize we have a national problem, almost a national emergency . . . on our hands. This is no longer a departmental problem, where one department fights it out with another department, nor is it a legislative-versus-executive fight."

Halaby, himself a pilot with many years of experience, added something that only pilots had been able to recognize at that point. "Airplanes are going so fast now," he said, "that there is literally not time, even though they see each other as much as a mile away, to avoid each other. It is just not physically possible."

That, too, was a product of the Jet Age, but one that had not yet made headlines and that did not figure in the advertising of the fantastic new flight schedules now possible. But aviation writer Rod Serling pointed it out in terms even more dramatic than Najeeb Halaby's. Two jet liners at cruising altitude, he wrote, are traveling 500 or 600 miles per hour. That is the speed at which a bullet blasts out of the muzzle of a .45-calibre automatic when the trigger is pulled. If two jet aircraft see they are approaching each other head-on at such a speed, they are really doomed. From the moment they first spot each other, there is no time for them to avoid each other. The only way that flying can be made safe in the Jet Age—the *only* way—is to keep these two airplanes apart, to make sure they are never on converging courses. As one aircraft controller told me not long ago: "Separation is the name of the game."

Chapter 8
Midair Collision

June 30, 1956. Two airliners were in the final stages of boarding at Los Angeles International Airport. TWA's Flight 2, a Lockheed Super-Constellation, was carrying 64 passengers to Kansas City. United Airlines Flight 718, a Douglas DC-7, had 53 people aboard and was bound for Chicago. The sky at Los Angeles was heavily overcast and both airplanes had filed Instrument Flight Plans. The Constellation would be cruising at 19,000 feet, the DC-7 at 21,000. The DC-7's course took it over Palm Springs; the Constellation was flying a more northerly route.

For most of their trip the two airplanes would be many miles apart. Only at the Grand Canyon did the tracks converge. By the time the airplanes reached that point, they were expected to be well apart horizontally due to differences in their speeds, and, in any event, they were separated vertically by 2,000 feet of altitude.

The two airplanes took off within three minutes of each other. Within an hour they were above the overcast and flying by visual flight rules, on the principle of "see and be seen." Both planes were also flying "off airways," avoiding the zigs and zags of airways laid out to touch as many localities as possible—a standard practice on long-distance flights.

The planes were thus beyond the reach of the ground controllers at their radar sets below. They would, however, make regular reports as they passed checkpoints below so that ground controllers would be able to keep track of their progress. One ground controller noted the estimated arrival time of the two airlines over the checkpoint at Grand Canyon: 10:34. Busy with other flights, he made no note of the coincidence: the time was identical for both aircraft.

At 10:31 the two airplanes collied right over the Grand Canyon.

Exactly what happened will never be known, because nobody survived the crash. Locked together, the wreckage of the Super-Constellation and the DC-7 spun for some 20,000 feet into a part of the Grand Canyon so inaccessible that only helicopters could get in to rescue what was left of the passengers and planes.

This much was clear, however: amazingly, the two planes had kept pace with each other on their different courses all the way from Los Angeles, so that at the point where their tracks converged, the Constellation, cruising at about 270 knots, was being slowly over-taken by the DC-7, which was making about 288 knots. The DC-7, cleared from the start for a higher altitude, was flying slightly above the Constellation. Each airplane was thus almost precisely in the other's "blind spot": the DC-7 pilot could not see down and past his nose well enough to spot the plane below him, and the pilot of the Constellation could have seen the overtaking craft only by craning his neck to see back and up out of his side window. Voice transmissions monitored by ground stations indicate that in the last seconds the crews did see the impending collision. "Up! Up! We're going in . . . " were the last words heard from the stricken craft.

The impact of this accident on the nation was stunning. The circumstances alone were dramatic enough: a crash in clear, un-crowded skies over a wilderness like the Grand Canyon. Even more astounding was the fact that it could have happened at all. As one aviation writer put it, this was the "impossible" accident, but he would probably have had some trouble getting pilots to agree with him on that, pilots being well aware of the many shortcomings of the air traffic control system.

Perhaps most astonishing to the public—and also to the members of Congress who for so many years had gone along with the austerity programs that straitjacketed the FAA—was the fact that there was no device to warn aircraft of impending collisions. Edward P. Curtis, Eisenhower's Special Assistant for Aviation Facilities Planning, told Congress that there was no electronic warning device then in existence that could have prevented the collision. Not even radar, he said, had "reached a point where [it] could be of real, practical use" in such a situation.

The Civil Aeronautics Administration disclaimed any responsibility. The two planes were flying in uncontrolled airspace, hence no civil air regulations were involved. In other words, they were flying under the laws of Lindbergh's time. But why was there not a direct, controlled, transcontinental route out of Los Angeles? "Funds, personnel, and equipment," was the reply. It was pointed out that the civil airways were laid out for short hauls because that is where the bulk of the traffic was.

All of the horror, all of the outrage, all of the talk finally did some good. The CAA, which to many might have seemed to be ducking the issue of responsibility, actually already had up its sleeve the kind of plan that could have prevented the Grand Canyon disaster. It was a five-year plan to modernize the airways and traffic control system, which called for an expenditure of nearly $250 million to buy and install radar, communications, and navigation aids all along the federal airways system. Included were 69 long-range radars, almost twice the number then in existence, close to 400 VORs (omnidirectional radio beacons) and 40 new airport towers for local traffic control. Within a year, the CAA expected to control all airspace above 24,000 feet and, as more radars were added, to lower this progressively until all airspace above 15,000 feet was under control from the ground.

Congress was in no mood to twiddle its thumbs. When the five-year plan came up for discussion, it was changed into a three-year plan, and more money was added to provide more radar, more VORs, and more airport surveillance facilities.

Still, despite the fact that the Grand Canyon crash had finally awakened the nation and the Congress to the urgent needs of air traffic control, there remained one nagging question that, even when all the radar sets and VORs and traffic controllers were in place, continued to haunt American aviation: the problem of an effective collision avoidance system. The fiftieth anniversary of the Wright brothers' first flight had gone. A quarter-century had passed since the first beginnings of organized aviation in America. There were all kinds of electronic gear sprouting up and down the airways. Why, in that case, was there nothing that could prevent airplanes from hitting each other in midair?

Actually, the problem is more complex than it seems. The greatest danger of collisions is in and around airports, where congestion is thickest because all incoming planes are being drawn, as in a funnel, to the common target of the runway. Collisions in the air can come from any direction, so a collision-warning device must be

79

able to "see" the impending danger from all sides: ahead, behind, above, below, from one side or from the other. Not only that, it must also make instantly apparent to the pilot where the danger is coming from so that he can take appropriate evasive action. At airplane speeds, there is no time for neckcraning and peering about: action must be instantaneous. The airplane has to be surrounded with a sort of invisible shroud that will fly with it at all times and, when approached, will give immediate warning of impending danger.

A good example of how such a device might work is offered by the tragic midair collision in San Diego in October, 1978. In that case, a small Cessna was flying instrument landing patterns at San Diego's Lindbergh Field. In it were the pilot, who was sharpening his IFR (instrument flight rules) skills, and his instructor. Since it was on IFR, the Cessna was under full control of the San Diego tower, where a controller was following its every move on his radar scope.

Into Lindbergh Field on this brilliant sunny morning came a Pacific Southwest Airlines Boeing 727, loaded with passengers. It, too, was under positive control of the San Diego tower, as all airliners are these days. The 727 was advised of the presence of the Cessna, which was practicing landings at the field, and the Cessna was advised that the 727 was approaching and would land on the Lindbergh Field runway. Both pilots acknowledged the transmission; the 727 pilot, after a brief interval, radioed the tower to say that he had the Cessna in sight.

And yet, minutes later, the two planes collided. The airliner let down onto the Cessna, overtaking it from above and behind. The occupants of the Cessna probably died instantly. The wing tanks of the 727 burst into flame, and it nosed down sharply. Burning fiercely, it struck the earth in a housing settlement adjacent to the field. No one left the airliner alive.

The extraordinary aspect of this terrible collision was that everything in the plane and on the ground that had to do with air traffic control worked perfectly. Both planes were seen on radar, and their collision courses were predicted and made known to both pilots. Both pilots received the collision warning and acknowledged it. The computer in the tower shortly thereafter issued a "conflict alert," which caused the 727's blip and data block on the radar screen to flash repeatedly as a warning signal. This conflict alert, however, was not transmitted to the two converging aircraft: the controller, knowing that both had received the earlier warning signal and presumably had each other in sight, decided that the

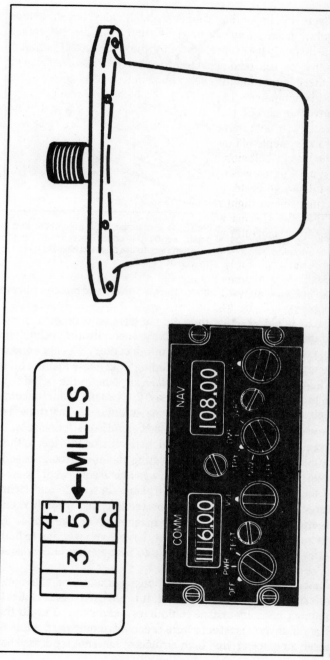

Distance Measuring Equipment (DME) is another magical black box that aids precise air navigation. It sends a VHF signal to the VORTAC facility tuned by the pilot. The time required for the signal to return to the aircraft is measured by computer and transformed into the straight-line distance in miles, then displayed on the instrument panel. The antenna (right) is placed beneath the aircraft.

81

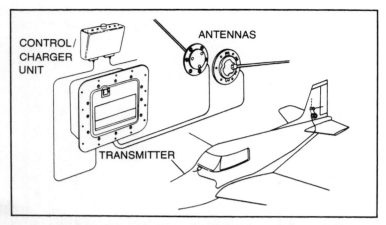

The Emergency Locator Transmitter (ELT) is a simple VHF transmitter that is designed to be activated by a crash, sending a continuous signal on the emergency frequency which will lead searchers to the downed aircraft. It works, sometimes.

better part of wisdom was to leave the two alone and not complicate their problem.

Well, it is obvious that they did not have each other in sight, and it is important to note that the most sophisticated technology that man could devise late in the twentieth century was not enough to prevent these two planes from colliding. It is likely that the pilot of the 727 was visually tracking *another* airplane in the belief that this was the danger plane and never saw the Cessna at all. It seems equally clear that the pilot of the Cessna, intent on his instruments, did not see the 727, which was above and behind in his "blind spot."

It certainly does seem that an anticollision device, either airborne and installed in the two conflicting planes or ground-based, could have prevented this accident. It was a case somewhat like the Grand Canyon crash of 1956: two airplanes in a wide and clear, uncluttered sky in CAVU conditions (ceiling and visibility un-limited) drawn together as though by magnets. A device that could sense an intruder plane would certainly have given warning to both pilots, who would then have been able to take appropriate evasive action.

Whether there will ever actually be a workable, reliable colli-sion avoidance system is a moot point. It is not particularly difficult to imagine an instrument that could have been used to avoid the 1956 Grand Canyon disaster, where there were miles and miles of uncluttered airspace around both airplanes; but another crash that occurred four years later over New York City posed totally different problems, and it is hard to see how a collision avoidance system could have been used to avoid this one.

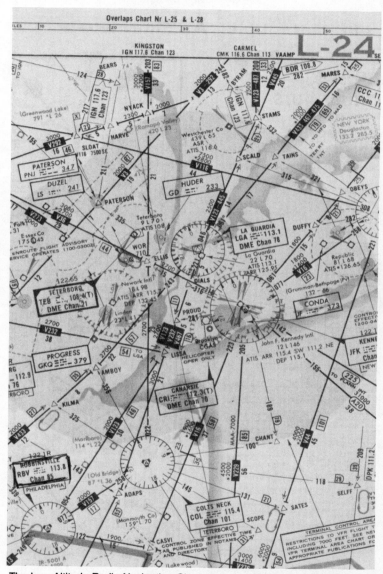

The Low Altitude Radio Navigation Chart shows no topographical features. La Guardia and Kennedy airports are in the center.

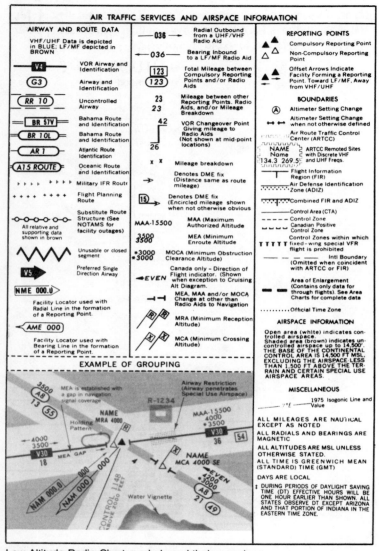

Low Altitude Radio Chart symbols and their meanings.

The airplanes involved were a United Airlines DC-8 jet, and a TWA Super-Constellation (ironically, both planes were flown by the same airlines that had been involved in the Grand Canyon crash). The Constellation was making a routine approach up the Hudson River to La Guardia Airport and was being guided in to its

L-23
PANELS ABCD
1"=12 NM

L-24
PANELS EFGH
1"=10 NM

UNITED STATES GOVERNMENT
FLIGHT INFORMATION PUBLICATION

ENROUTE LOW ALTITUDE – U.S.

For use up to but not including 18,000' MSL

L E G E N D

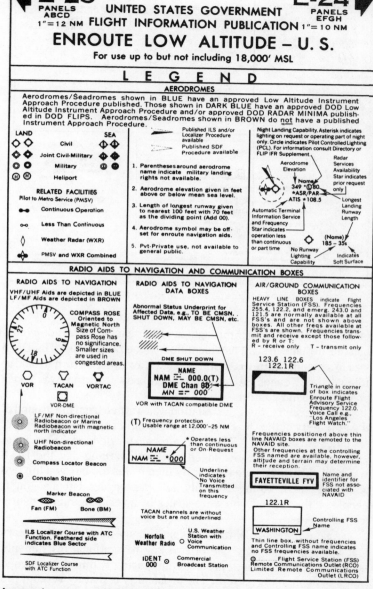

An amazing amount of information is contained in these En Route Low Altitude charts. The various air charts are so well done that they have made a significant contribution to air safety in the United States.

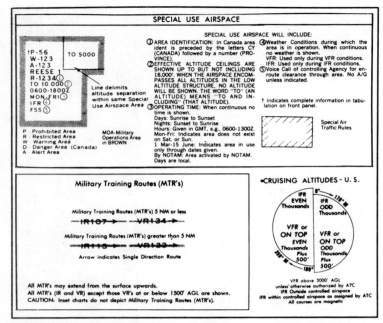

Additional data on the En Route Low Altitude (below 18,000 ft) Radio Navigation Charts.

landing by radar, which throughout the tragic sequence of events had the airplane in sight and identified on the radarscope. The DC-8 was in a holding pattern off Staten Island, awaiting its turn to land at Idlewild, as Kennedy Airport was then known. It, too, was under positive ground control.

Furthermore, the Constellation was warned from the ground of the proximity of the DC-8: "Unidentified target approaching you . . . six miles . . . jet traffic." The TWA pilot acknowledged the warning: "Roger." He also acknowledged a second warning that the DC-8 was now only three miles away. By then it was too late and the two planes crashed, killing not only 127 passengers but also eight people on the ground who were struck by a veritable rain of debris from the skies.

Again, the cause of this accident is conjectural, but it appears that the DC-8 had only one of two key navigational instruments operative, which created problems in staying within the assigned limits of the holding pattern. The probability is that it overshot the pattern and invaded the approach corridor to La Guardia, up which the TWA Constellation was proceeding. The rate of closure with

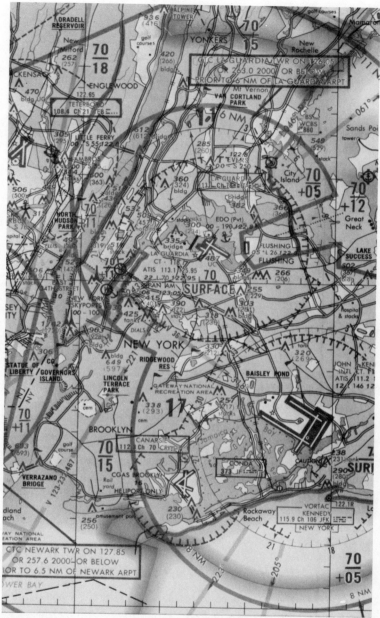

The VFR Terminal Area Charts are essential when navigating by visual flight rules into a TCA. Here, we are looking at a portion of the La Guardia and Kennedy Terminal Control Areas.

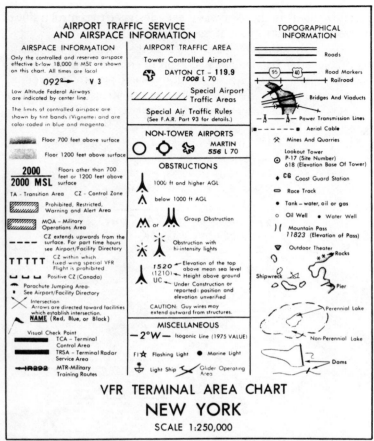

AIRPORT TRAFFIC SERVICE AND AIRSPACE INFORMATION

AIRSPACE INFORMATION

Only the controlled and reserved airspace effective below 18,000 ft MSL are shown on this chart. All times are local

092° **V 3**

Low Altitude Federal Airways are indicated by center line.

The limits of controlled airspace are shown by tint bands (Vignette) and are color-coded in blue and magenta.

Floor 700 feet above surface

Floor 1200 feet above surface

2000
2000 MSL Floors other than 700 feet or 1200 feet above surface

TA - Transition Area   CZ - Control Zone

Prohibited, Restricted, Warning and Alert Area

MOA — Military Operations Area

CZ extends upwards from the surface. For part time hours see Airport/Facility Directory

TTTTT CZ within which fixed wing special VFR Flight is prohibited

Positive CZ (Canada)

Parachute Jumping Area— See Airport/Facility Directory

Intersection
Arrows are directed toward facilities which establish intersection.
NAME (Red, Blue, or Black)

Visual Check Point

TCA — Terminal Control Area

TRSA — Terminal Radar Service Area

IR292 MTR-Military Training Routes

AIRPORT TRAFFIC AREA

Tower Controlled Airport

DAYTON CT – **119.9**
1008 L 70

Special Airport Traffic Areas

Special Air Traffic Rules
(See F.A.R. Part 93 for details.)

NON-TOWER AIRPORTS

○ ◇ ⊕ MARTIN
556 L 70

OBSTRUCTIONS

⋀ 1000 ft and higher AGL

⋀ below 1000 ft AGL

⋀ or ⋀⋀ Group Obstruction

⋇ Obstruction with hi-intensity lights

1520 ← Elevation of the top above mean sea level
(1210) ← Height above ground
UC ← Under Construction or reported: position and elevation unverified

CAUTION: Guy wires may extend outward from structures.

MISCELLANEOUS

—**2°W**— Isogonic Line (1975 VALUE)

Fl☆ Flashing Light   ● Marine Light

⚓ Light Ship   Glider Operating Area

TOPOGRAPHICAL INFORMATION

Roads

95 40 Road Markers
Railroad

Bridges And Viaducts

—Λ——Λ— Power Transmission Lines

Aerial Cable

✕ Mines And Quarries

Lookout Tower
P-17 (Site Number)
618 (Elevation Base Of Tower)

CG Coast Guard Station

Race Track

● Tank – water, oil or gas

○ Oil Well   ● Water Well

)(Mountain Pass
11823 (Elevation of Pass)

Outdoor Theater

Rocks

Shipwreck

Pier

Perennial Lake

Non-Perennial Lake

Dams

VFR TERMINAL AREA CHART
NEW YORK
SCALE 1:250,000

Keys to some of the airport and air traffic data contained in VFR Terminal Area Charts.

the Constellation was too great to permit any effective evasive action.

The problem of a collision avoidance system is still very much a priority, but in the meantime the dangers of collision have been dealt with in a different way. It is apt at this point to recall the parting words of FAA Administrator Elwood "Pete" Quesada, President Eisenhower's appointee who brought the FAA into the modern world during his tenure from 1953 to 1960: "Technically, the [traffic control] system . . . in use [when I assumed office] was much the same as that devised to accommodate the DC-3. It was never meant to cope with the complex patterns of civil and military traffic that now filled the sky. Nor was it ever designed to control traffic of high-speed aircraft flying at many altitudes."

Basically, things hadn't changed all that much—it was mainly that the system had been speeded up to some degree to keep up with the speed of the airplanes. But the same picture of keyed-up, overworked men at the radarscopes, of relentlessly moving blips and data blocks, each representing an airplane full of human beings, still prevailed in the air traffic control centers. The same pressures for funds and personnel still beset the FAA Administrator, except that now, in the face of the terrible tolls exacted by the crashes that did occur, the members of Congress were more amenable to the arguments that air safety could not be shoved under the table.

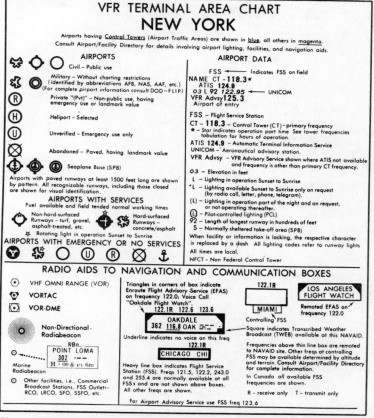

Airports, airport services, and radio frequencies, along with terrain features and prominent landmarks, are among the data provided by the VFR TAC Charts.

NEW YORK TERMINAL CONTROL AREA (GROUP 1)

See back of this chart for procedural
information within the New York Terminal Control Area (TCA)

70 -- Ceiling of TCA in hundreds of feet MSL

10 -- Floor of TCA in hundreds of feet MSL

(Floors extending "upward from above" a certain altitude are preceded by
a + Operations at and below these altitudes are outside of TCA).

CONTROL TOWER FREQUENCIES
ON NEW YORK VFR TERMINAL AREA CHART

Airports which have control towers are indicated on this chart by the letters CT followed by the
primary VHF local control frequency. Selected transmitting frequencies for each control tower are
tabulated in the adjoining spaces, the low or medium transmitting frequency is listed first
followed by a VHF local control frequency and the primary VHF and UHF military frequencies,
when these frequencies are available. An asterisk (*) follows the part time tower frequency
remoted to the collocated full time FSS for use as Airport Advisory Service (AAS) during hours
tower is closed. Receiving frequencies are shown thus: 122.5R. Hours shown are local time.

Automatic Terminal Information Service (ATIS) frequencies, shown on the face of the chart are
normal arriving frequencies, all ATIS frequencies available are tabulated below.

ASR and/or PAR indicates Radar Instrument Approach available.

```
ESSEX COUNTY ................ Opr 0800-2200 ....................... 126.5
(Caldwell Twr)
GRUMMAN BETHPAGE NF ........ Opr 0800-1630 ............. 121.3 126.2 340.2
(Bethpage Twr)            Mon-Fri
JOHN F KENNEDY INTL ......... ATIS Arr 111.2 115.4 ................. 119.1 258.3
(Kennedy Twr)            Dep 115.1
LA GUARDIA ................. ATIS Arr & Dep 113.1 ................. 118.7 263.0
                         Arr 125.95
LONG ISLAND MACARTHUR ........ ATIS 128.45 ..................... 119.3 233.2
(Long Island Twr)
TRSA: 124.05 239.3 (Within 10 NM)
      120.05 239.3 (Beyond 10 NM)
MERCER CO (Trenton Twr) .......... ATIS 119.45 ................. 120.7 257.8

MORRISTOWN ... ATIS 124.25 ............ Opr 0630-2230 ........... 118.1 353.9

NEWARK INTL ............ ATIS Arr 115.7 Dep 132.45 .............. 118.3 257.6

REPUBLIC ... ATIS 126.65 ........ Opr 0700-2300 .............. 118.8 229.5

SIKORSKY HELIPORT NF ......... Opr 0800-1600 ................... 123.2 314.6
                         Mon-Fri
SIKORSKY MEM (Bridgeport Twr) .... Opr 0700-2300 .................. 120.9 257.8

TETERBORO .................... ATIS 108.4 .................... 119.5 125.1

WESTCHESTER CO ............... ATIS 116.6 ........... 119.7 126.75 381.2 ASR
```

Published at Washington, D.C.
U.S. Department of Commerce
National Oceanic and Atmospheric Administration
National Ocean Survey

The National Oceananic and Atmospheric Administration (NOAA) produces all
FAA air charts, and all are up-dated frequently.

The modern general aviation pilot flies more complicated machines in a more complex environment than did his or her counterpart of a generation ago, and the requirements for stepping-up from single-engine to multiengine aircraft include an impressive ground study course (above) as well as additional dual flight instruction.

The FAA itself had grown into a major agency. By the end of 1960 it was spending some $300 million per year to operate more than 9,500 navigation and traffic control facilities. New facilities and equipment added $120 million annually to that total—ten times the amount spent on new equipment when Quesada came into office. The FAA administered 425 flight service stations, which were in communication with aircraft en route along the airways; 288 airport control towers, 41 long-range radars and 21 precision approach radars; 53 airport surveillance radars; and 35 air route traffic control centers.

It was an impressive array, but it was not enough. Nor was it enough to simply add more to that which already existed—airports in particular were approaching the saturation point. A new concept was needed, and a new concept was waiting in the wings. The word for it was *separation*—not just separation in terms of airspace, but separation of aircraft among themselves: what some bitter spokesmen for general aviation would call *segregation*.

Chapter 9
Positive Control

In no other country in the world can one see the number and diversity of airplanes that populate the skies and the airports of the United States. Eugene Vidal's old idea of a "flivver" plane has come closer to reality in this country than anywhere else: there actually are families where both parents are pilots and they take the kids up for Sunday outings or flying vacations to someplace far away. It may start with a boy of 16 who builds an ultralight fitted with a chainsaw engine; it may end up with a Beechcraft Baron.

There are close to 400,000 general aviation airplanes operating in the United States, and they range in size all the way from two-seater Cessna 150s to Grumman Gulfstreams, Learjets, and a wide range of similar corporate aircraft. The speed differential between these various airplanes may be as much as 400 miles per hour. Yet each of these aircraft, when the day's flying is done, has to have a runway on which to land and an approach corridor to reach that runway—and it is here that trouble begins.

Few words are more compelling to the ear of a private pilot in a small, slow airplane on final approach than the tower's admonition: "Piper One-Three-Delta, please expedite approach; there's a Gulfstream on your tail." What to do? It isn't like being in an automobile, where you can step on the gas and speed up. A landing airplane has a prescribed approach speed, and if the throttle is pushed forward and the control yoke pushed ahead to accelerate matters, then the plane reaches the runway going too fast. No, it is

Since about half of all inter-city air travel in the United States is flown in general aviation aircraft, it is apparent that general aviation and the commercial air carriers complement one another. There can be no question as to which half is the more important; the two must coexist.

A recent and (at this writing) still unregulated factor in aviation is the proliferation of the ultralight aircraft. These are fun machines, inexpensive to own and fly. Surely, these free spirits have a place in the skies, but unlicensed pilots, without radios and obligations to air regulations, cannot mix with other air traffic.

The Gates Learjet, certified by the FAA to operate up to 51,000 feet, exceeds the structural standards established for airliners. It is a business machine, primarily owned by large corporations to increase the effectiveness of key personnel.

the pilot of the big, faster plane who should be called upon to slow up his approach by serpentine maneuvers or other means. But that's not the way the world works; man tends to equate bigness with importance, and so the pilot of the little airplane gets the heat, and when he sees what's bearing down on him from behind, he may well know apprehension.

How to cope with this mix of large and small, fast and slow airplanes at the nation's air terminals? The problem, after nearly half a century, still plagues aviation in America. As big as the skies seem to be, they shrink when filled up with 500-mile-per-hour jet airliners and Mach 2 military aircraft, and with 150-mile-per-hour Pipers, Cessnas, Mooneys, and all the other small, private planes. One Piper Tripacer flying down the final approach lane toward its 65-mile-per-hour landing takes up the same space that could be used to land a jet airliner, which comes down at almost twice the speed. Air controllers, who hold all those lives in their hands, have to think in terms of generous envelopes of protective space around all the aircraft that come into their area.

On April 21, 1958, at Las Vegas, Nevada, in the brilliantly clear, unpolluted skies for which the desert is famous, a DC-7 was hit squarely and completely unexpectedly by an Air Force jet fighter screaming down in a flat-out power dive for Nellis Air Force Base below. The accident occurred at 21,000 feet, so it is superfluous to say there were no survivors. The fighter was going so fast that "see and be seen" never had a chance to work, and 49 people were killed.

Ironically, on that very day the Civil Aeronautics Board was meeting to consider a plan for "positive control" of flights within designated airspace. The plan had been worked out by Oscar Bakke, head of the CAB's Bureau of Safety Regulation. It may come as a surprise to hear that many persons in the aviation community devoutly hoped it would never see the light of day. What Bakke wanted to institute was a system that would put aircraft operating along certain airways under the control of radar operators on the ground; these would be able to see what other aircraft were in the same general area and thus keep them from running into each other. The fighter at Las Vegas, for example, might have been told "no diving here; too much traffic," or the DC-7 might have been warned that "there's a fighter diving through your airspace; make immediate right turn to avoid him."

What was wrong with that idea? It was the old bugaboo of freedom rearing its head again, and once again in the wrong place. General aviation saw it as another regulation to add to the many that were forcing the private airplane out of the skies. Many airline pilots saw it as an infringement on their authority in the cockpit: they did not want to have to do whatever a ground controller told them they should do. The military were against it because they felt that, more than anyone, they had priority in the struggle for freedom of the skies.

Yet, in the end, nobody could come up with a better way of preventing such terrifying disasters as the Las Vegas crash, which could easily have been avoided. The very thought that Nellis Air Force Base, from which nearly 200 military airplanes took off every day, could operate in total ignorance of what was going on along a heavily traveled airway directly overhead was enough to anger any airline passenger who knew about it. And Nellis was not an exceptional case. A month after the Las Vegas crash, in a startling replay near Brunswick, Maryland, a Capital Viscount airliner was hit by a National Guard jet; the result was 12 people dead.

Positive control is another way of spelling "separation," and separation is the only practical way to keep airplanes from colliding with each other in midair. What it means is that ground controllers watching their radar screens can monitor the distance, both vertical (altitude) and horizontal (miles) separating the airplanes they see there. If two planes get too close horizontally, one can be told to speed up, slow down, turn to one side or the other—whatever is necessary to avoid danger. They can be kept at different altitudes, too. And, as they approach their destination airport, they can be formed into a paradelike line before the hand-off to the airport control tower, thus avoiding overcrowding on the approach lanes.

But, like everything in the three-dimensional medium of the air, positive control has its complications too. What, exactly, should it seek to accomplish? Where should it begin? How high should it extend? How low? And who should be covered?

The first attempt to answer these questions simply proved how difficult they were. Positive control meant precise instrument flying along designated airways. At first three transcontinental routes were so designated between 17,000 and 22,000 feet. In these airways VFR flight was banned. The military, conceding the futility of controlling one part of aviation without controlling the other, agreed to accept positive Civil Aeronautics Administration control on all "nontactical" jet flights under 20,000 feet. This enormously reduced the risk of civilian and military entanglements along the airways. Perhaps even more comforting to the airline pilots was the Air Force's assurance that there would be no more high-speed dives through congested areas to airports.

A Delta Air Lines Lockheed L-1011 Tristar, fitted with Rolls-Royce turbofan engines, is representative of the wide-bodied airliners currently in service.

As for the airlines, they opted to fly on instruments whenever at altitudes above 18,000 feet, which meant that at cruising altitudes they would no longer use "see and be seen," but would accept the CAA's positive control. By the end of 1959, they planned to lower the "floor" for IFR flight to 10,000 feet.

So far so good; it was a minor revolution but one well worth celebrating. The military and the airlines had accepted the CAB's thinking. Still opposition remained on the part of general aviation and was expressed by the Aircraft Owners and Pilots Association (AOPA).

General Elwood "Pete" Quesada, President Eisenhower's favored aviation expert and former CAA Administrator, put the whole matter in perspective when he said: "Positive control is still a decade away. This is the blunt fact that must be faced by all concerned with air safety. Because not enough has been done in the past, the future has caught up with us before we are ready. Problems in the making for 20 years are not going to be solved overnight." Senator A.S. "Mike" Monroney seconded Quesada's prediction that at some point military and civilian traffic would have to be integrated and pointed out the chilling fact that the control tower at Las Vegas Airport and at Nellis Air Force Base were only six miles apart, yet they had absolutely no contact whatsoever. "The right hand does not know what the left hand is doing," he observed. "Such a situation is almost as dangerous as a busy intersection at which the red lights [are] supervised by one agency and the green lights by another."

As for the ground controllers, despite a shortage of radar sets, manpower, and money, they quickly found themselves handling twice as much traffic as before. Within a year the number of departures from air traffic control centers had doubled, to 3 million. The new system proved to be expensive in an unexpected way: it took longer to travel under positive control than under the old laissez faire system. Coast-to-coast flights were losing 44 minutes on the average on round trips, and, in a highly competitive business, this looked like a lot of time on an airline schedule.

Nonetheless, the epidemic of crashes and near-misses, which had done so much to support the concept of positive control, seemed to have been halted. By the end of the 1950s, the United States had entered the Jet Age in relative peace and safety, and Boeing 707s, Douglas DC-8s, and six-hour flights to Europe were accepted facts. Yet, astonishingly, air safety had been secured for less than 20 percent of America's air fleet. This was because positive control had not yet been instituted at low altitudes in the high-density areas around airports. This meant that *most* of America's airplanes—for which read all airplanes categorized as "general aviation"—still flew VFR. "The eyeball is not obsolete!" gloated the AOPA. Clarence Sayen, president of the Airline Pilots Association, told Senator Monroney's Subcommittee on Aviation that approximately 85 percent of all air activity was still conducted under visual flight rules (VFR). "With all its acknowledged deficiencies, 'see and be seen' is still the prime system. This," he added, "is far from being a satisfactory situation."

However, recognizing this and doing something about it were still two entirely different matters. The best, the most diligent, the most dedicated planners time and again came to grief on the complexity of aviation's problems. Every facet of the industry—the planes themselves, the men who built them, the men who flew them, the passengers who rode in them, the government that tried to regulate them—seemed capable, like Hydra, growing multiple new heads each time a problem was solved. And in the 1960s the monster head that most confounded the experts was the growth of aviation itself.

In 1963 there were 87,267 airplanes flying in American skies. Four years later, in 1967, there were 116, 794: an increase of 33 percent. Nobody had—nor could have—anticipated a jump like that. Licensed airmen in the United States increased from 268,819 in 1963 to 429,364 in 1967: a jump of nearly 60 percent. In that same time the number of takeoffs and landings monitored by airport control towers increased by 54 percent, and the number of people carried by the airlines almost doubled. Jets accounted for most of that: they could carry more people on more trips while themselves increasing in number by only a relatively modest 24 percent.

In scheduled airline service, piston-powered aircraft were scarcely seen. Super-Constellations, Stratoliners, and DC-7s were obsolete.

The problem of the sheer number of airplanes was bad enough, but there was another problem within that one. The increase in flying and in people who flew was not evenly distributed. It centered, for the most part, on New York, Los Angeles, Chicago, and Washington, D.C. At these largest of the nation's terminals, 29 percent of the increase jockeyed for space on the runways. La Guardia Airport in New York almost *doubled* its traffic, registering a growth rate of 96 percent. And, of course, crowded as they were in the restricted space available, the airlines jostled each other even more by scheduling most of their flights in the peak hours, when the most people wanted to fly.

It was no different with general aviation. The Pipers, the Cessnas, the Beechcraft, and the larger AeroCommanders, Gulfstreams, Learjets, and Convairs blossomed like flowers in the spring. And, of course, waving their well-known perrogative of freedom of the skies, they too joined the throng vying for space at the airports. Only now there was one big difference that had not existed before between them and the airliners: the speed differential between, say, a Piper Tripacer coming in for a landing and a four-engine Boeing 707 returning from a round trip to Paris. The Tripacer's *top* speed was still slower than the 707's *minimum* speed, and this mixture of slow and fast, large and small turned the controller's always-taxing job into a veritable nightmare.

One solution, of course, was to find other airports for general aviation to use. In Washington, D.C., there was one right across the river from the dangerously overtaxed National Airport. This was the Anacostia Naval Air Station and Bolling Air Force Base.

General William F. McKee, FAA Administrator, saw Anacostia-Bolling as the perfect solution to the general aviation problem at Washington National, and without any difficulty succeeded in getting the agreement of Vice President Hubert Humphrey and of Mendel Rivers, chairman of the House Armed Services Committee, for his plan to have the runways there made available on a temporary basis until a permanent solution could be worked out. But President Lyndon Johnson had other ideas. He wanted general aviation to use Dulles Airport, the beautiful new facility far out beyond the Washington suburbs, which at this point was used only for overseas arrivals and departures. He was not to be moved. McKee had no authority to divert general aviation to Dulles, and he could foresee a bitter outcry against attempt to do so. Passengers at Washington National, therefore, went on risking their necks, knowingly or unknowingly, every time they flew there.

The tremendous overcrowding at Washington National was, in a way, symptomatic of the problem faced everywhere in the nation. No matter what was done, the overcrowding on the airports and on their approaches never seemed to get better and frequently got worse. General McKee finally put his finger on the heart of the matter. "Suddenly it was clear," he said, "that we were getting behind, and that's when we started the fight to get the resources necessary to catch up."

There must be something about being safely on the ground that

Today's air navigation aids and weather reporting network make night flying routine, a far cry from the navigation-by-bonfire practiced by the early airmail pilots.

makes the risk of being high up in the air seem very theoretical to many persons, particularly to politicians. The history of regulating flight for safety's sake in the United States is like a ride through a turbulent sky: up (usually after a bad series of crashes have awakened public indignation) and down (when the stresses of budget discussions take precedence over awareness of danger). So it continued through most of the 1960s, with General McKee, like his predecessors, fighting for funds to buy radar sets and install them, to hire new personnel and train them, and to build new facilities at terminals and along the airways and man them. And above, in the high skies the airplanes continued to fly with their increasing loads of passengers, whose apprehensions as well as numbers grew.

When President Johnson made his dramatic departure from office and Richard Nixon was elected to succeed him in 1969, an effort was made to bring some financial stability to air safety. The Airport and Airway Development Acts combined user taxes, head taxes, excise taxes, state taxes, and federal matching grants in such a manner that it was possible, in theory at least, for the FAA to stay ahead of the game. Money was available not only to procure the necessary hardware to run the show efficiently but also to anticipate future needs by engaging in forward-looking research that would keep the FAA abreast of new developments. It was this sort of thing that finally brought long-range radar to the airways together with the alphanumerics data system (the data blocks on the radar screen which identify airplanes and give their height, course, and speed).

High-altitude positive control also came into general use. At first limited to the airways, it soon was also applied to terminal areas, on the crowded approach and departure lanes where it was most needed. Terminal Control Areas (TCAs) were gradually put into effect all across the country, walling off large areas around major airports to all but suitably equipped (transponders were mandatory) aircraft. The expected outcry was instantly forthcoming, but the urgency of taking such measures to protect the lives of thousands of airline passengers could no longer be denied.

Separation was, more than ever, the name of the game. Each passenger airplane had to be surrounded by an absolutely inviolable blanket of protective distance, and the only men who could assure this were the ground controllers in front of their radar sets. With each new measure, the pressure on them grew, until at last they decided to organize into a union that could speak for them and make known when the burden of their constant surveillance became too great. This brought into the already complicated picture an entirely new force with which to contend.

Another important function of general aviation is air ambulance service

The Beechcraft Super King Air is the leading propjet operated by American corporations.

Meanwhile, work went on to develop the next generation of hardware for the promotion of the air safety. At the top of the list was still the anticollision device, the obvious cure-all for that most dreaded of flying emergencies, the midair collision. The aircraft, too, were coming under the closest FAA scrutiny in an effort to improve their "crash-worthiness" and thereby save the lives of passengers who might survive an accident but still be killed inside the airplane because they could not get out (many a plane has managed to come to earth relatively intact only to lose most or all of its passengers when fire breaks out and they are trapped inside the cabin).

Perhaps most promising for protection in the congested airport terminal area is the research going on to develop a microwave landing system. In simplified terms, such a system would surround the airport and a large area around it (the TCA) with a microwave grid into which the airplane's own controls would be locked as it approached. From then on, human interference would be minimal; even the ground controller's work would be greatly reduced. Computer-generated microwave signals would guide the airplane safely through the necessary maneuvers that put it on the proper glide path to the runway. It would be steered safely around other traffic and, once on the glide path, be brought down to a completely automatic landing. Such landings are, in fact, already possible. Weather makes no difference to the system, but it has to be rigorously exclusive: only airplanes properly announced, expected, equipped, and identified can be allowed into the terminal area and locked into the letdown system. The principle of separation to avoid collision will have to be accepted in the interest of safety.

In the long run, separation will probably divide general aviation from commercial aviation to the degree that the two will end up using separate airports. The best answer yet found to the question of mixing small and large, slow and fast airplanes is the satellite airport for general aviation. In Los Angeles, for example, it could be Orange County Airport; in the New York area it could be Teterboro in New Jersey or Westchester County Airport on the Connecticut-New York line. Parkways, bus, and helicopter service are available from such places into the city, and all services are right on hand for servicing and maintaining airplanes.

Chapter 10
Airborne Collision
Avoidance

Captain John Masters,* pilot and chief officer of Quantum Airlines Flight 37, sat in the command seat of his big Lockheed L-1011, staring our past its nose at the cloud-hung sky. At 11,000 feet the wide-bodied jet was just below the ceiling, with occasional ragged streamers of cloud whipping past in silent explosions of mist and rain. Far below, the fields, forests, highways, and villages of southern New Jersey filed past in solemn review, remote reminders of life on earth. The big jet was approaching the Omni beacon at Robbinsville, some 150 miles southwest of New York, and the steady, musical dot-dash signal—the only sound in the quiet cockpit—was comforting reassurance that Flight 37 was on course and that all was well.

Jim Hagert, the copilot, was on the controls. His eyes were fixed on the Omni course indicator, where the white needle hung precisely between the blue and yellow fields. Keeping that needle dead center would unfailingly bring them right over the beacon itself, where the needle would make a sudden wide swing right off the gauge, and a little sign on the display would change from *TO* to *FROM*. It would then be time to switch the navigational radio receiver from 067, the radial along which they had been flying to

---

*The names of all persons involved in this account have been changed to protect their privacy. The incident described, however, actually took place, and the details of how it happened are given as they occurred.

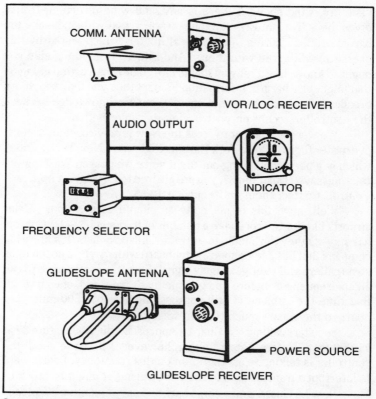

Component diagram of an Instrument Landing System (ILS).

Robbinsville, to 054, the outboard Robbinsville radial that would take them straight to New York.

"It was a nice, peaceful morning," Captain Masters said later, recalling the flight. "It was one of those calm, cloudy days with a high ceiling and now and then a bit of rain, a relaxing day when nothing seems really urgent. That's what makes that other fellow's behavior so difficult to understand.

"Well, we left Robbinsville on the 054 degree radial and I started getting ready for the various chores we would have to perform when we were approaching our landing. And the first thing I did was to tune in La Guardia and get Information Foxtrot.

"Information Foxtrot" is an important broadcast to any airplane coming in to land at La Guardia. It is an automatic, taped broadcast, and it repeats itself over and over, giving the weather at the airport—whether it's raining or not, the cloud ceiling, forward visibility, wind speed if there is any, and wind direction. It also gives the active runway—the one on which you will land—and the barometric pressure so that your altimeter (which works by this pressure) will agree with theirs. And if there is anything else you ought to know, like a runway that is closed or construction going on that might be a hazard, Information Foxtrot tells you that, too. It is a broadcast you must have and one you must acknowledge because the controllers count on your having that information.

"We were now about to cross the New Jersey coast for a short, overwater flight to New York Harbor. Right here New York Center, which had been controlling our flight since we passed Washington, calls and says: 'Quantum 37, you are cleared to La Guardia Approach Control. Contact them on frequency 120.8.'

"Well, now, this is not quite as simple as it sounds. Major airports like La Guardia have a number of frequencies—La Guardia has six—so they can handle their traffic with no delays. It's like a big company that has a telephone switchboard with maybe a dozen lines so no callers will ever get a busy signal. Sometimes you have to call all six frequencies before you get one that's free, and, of course, all that time the airplane is still approaching at about 500 miles per hour, so there isn't much time to waste.

"So I start calling: 'La Guardia Approach, this is Quantum 37 at 11,000 feet.' Before I start talking, however, I listen to see if the controller is talking to another pilot on that frequency. I don't want to interrupt a transmission to another airplane; it might be crucial.

"Now La Guardia may come back and say, 'Quantum 37, please

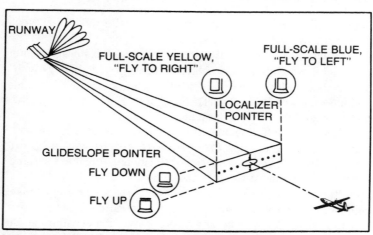

Indicators provided to the pilot utilizing an ILS approach.

indent,' which is short for 'identify.' This does not mean that they doubt my word as to who I am; it means they want more details. So I press my 'Ident' button and my transponder sends them the airline name and flight number, altitude, and speed. These now appear in the 'data block' which shows up on the radar screen right next to the blip that is my airplane. So now we are checked in and identified.

"The next message I get is 'Quantum 37, you are cleared to 8,000.' I motion to the copilot to go down, and we gradually lose 3,000 feet of altitude. But there is more to it than that—there is a speed limit of 250 knots below 10,000 feet, so Jim has to slow the airplane down and I must put on first flaps to keep it flying properly at the slower speed.

"Next the controller asks us to take up a heading of 45 degrees. We have crossed the water now and this course will take us right up the Hudson River. This will spare the folks below some of the noise a jet makes as it flies by. We get to be very conscious of this noise because so many of the maneuvers we are asked to make are dictated by it.

"As we fly up the Hudson we are cleared to successively lower altitudes and slower speeds, so that we have to pay close attention to the flaps and the airspeed. Because of the noise, the controllers try to keep us as high as possible for as long as possible, but we do have to come down eventually. They also try to keep us over water and away from residential areas.

"We have now crossed the George Washington Bridge and are flying up toward Yonkers, and here I am handed off to another controller who will take us all the way to La Guardia. He turns us to a heading of 120 degrees, which is southeastward and which is also the base leg for our approach to La Guardia. And it is right here, just about over City Island, that it happens.

"Fortunately I am looking out ahead at this point, not for anything in particular, but just looking. Jim still has his eyes on the instruments, as he should have. Our flight engineer is bent over the approach charts spread out on his little table. So I am the only one who has eyes ahead.

"I see it all of a sudden. It is straight in front of us, on the level of my eyes. It is an airplane. It has a single engine, white wings, and a dark body of some color I don't remember. The wings are straight and level, and it is coming toward us at more than a hundred miles per hour, while we are flying toward it at 250. So, our combined closing speed is more than 350 miles per hour, and he is less than a mile away.

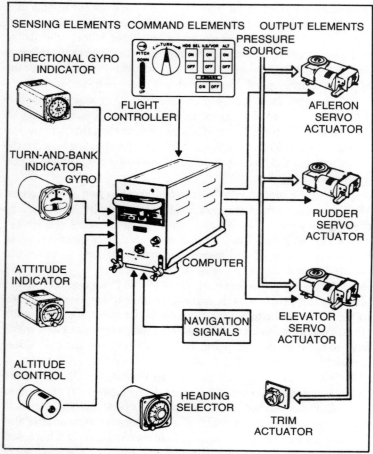

Components of an automatic pilot system.

"We cannot turn or dive our big airplane; it is already too late. But suddenly I see him climb and turn in one motion. He must have thrown the wheel over and pulled it right back into his stomach, and his airplane, which is light and nimble, is able to respond in time.

"The dark belly of the airplane and the gleaming white of its wings seem to be burned into my eyes as he flashes past. The whole thing is over so fast that it does not seem possible that it ever happened, but that burned-in picture is still there, proving that it did. It might have been one second—certainly less than two—from the moment I first saw him to the moment he flashed by, perhaps 50 feet away. 'What was that?' asked Jim—he never saw it at all. But the flight engineer did, and he let loose a string of curses at the pilot, whoever he might be. As for me, I immediately got on the radio and reported to La Guardia that there was a small airplane stooging around where we were. 'Okay, thanks,' the controller said after a brief search of his radar scope. 'I think I have him now.' And he cleared all the airplanes coming behind us to higher altitudes, since it seemed very unlikely that the little plane, which had probably lost its way, would climb up into the cloud cover.

"Of course, there was an investigation, and it was not until then that we found out what had happened. The small plane had taken off from Westchester County Airport about 25 miles to the north. He had filed a VFR flight plan for a trip to the west, but he got disoriented when he flew unexpectedly into clouds. When he broke out and saw water below him, he thought he was crossing the Hudson up around Hastings or Dobbs Ferry. Why? Because that is what he was looking for and hoped to see. Actually, he was in the completely opposite direction, crossing the shore of Long Island Sound at City Island. He probably never looked at his compass to confirm the direction he thought he was flying."

Flight 37, with Jim Hagert still flying, went on to complete an uneventful landing at La Guardia. The pilot of the "danger plane" went on to his western destination, from which, at the request of the FAA, he subsequently filed a detailed report on the near-miss. Among other things, it was evident that he had suffered from a rather severe case of what is known in the profession as "let's-go-anyway-itis," which had led him to take off into almost certain IFR weather without sufficient IFR skills.

Thinking about a story like Captain Masters' near-disaster, the question naturally arises: how could something like this happen at a time and under conditions in which all airplanes are as tightly controlled as they are in the immediate vicinity of La Guardia Airport? The answer is not very easy to come by, but the question strikes at the heart of the most important problem facing the FAA today: the development of a device that will make collisions between airplanes in the air impossible.

Prototypes of a anticollision system have already been tested, not only by the companies responsible for their development but by the FAA itself. Nothing as yet has turned up, but there are some systems that are pretty close. We shall examine these in due course, because it is safe enough to say that one such system will probably be operating in commercial aircraft within the next few years.

First of all, however, it is important to be realistic about our expectations and to consider what these devices will do and will not do.

They will doubtless be able to avoid collisions between commercial aircraft (airliners) because it is safe to say that all airliners will be plugged into the system, once it has been certified by the FAA. One cannot predict the same thing for general aviation. A large segment of general aviation consists of doctors, lawyers, farmers, small-business men, and flight students who do not have the means to install the latest word in technology in their airplanes. Moreover, they have their own powerful spokesman, the Aircraft Owners and Pilots Association to make known their wishes to both the FAA and Congress and to fight off legislation with which they might not want to comply. It is therefore doubtful whether, in the foreseeable future, there will ever be a time when it may safely be said that *every* airplane in the sky is plugged into an anticollision system.

The other problem is that of "unwanted alerts." The job of an anticollision device is to alert the pilot immediately, and without fail, to imminent danger, and to do this it has to make some sort of a loud noise, or shake the control wheel violently, or do something else to draw his attention. En route between cities there is not much chance of an "unwanted alert" because anything at cruising altitude is likely to be dangerous; but nearing the airport, where the traffic is at its most dense, an anticollision device can be set off by any number of nonthreatening aircraft. The pilot, pestered out of his wits by the constant signals signifying nothing, is likely to turn the device off just at the point where he needs it most.

Solving these two problems is not easy. Research has been proceeding actively on anticollision systems for a quarter of a century, ever since the Air Transport Association requested industry to produce or propose such a system. By 1976 three devices came out of this research: a McDonald-Douglas concept called, incongruously, EROS, or the Time/Frequency Airborne Collision Avoidance System; an RCA device called SECANT, for Separation and Control of Aircraft using Nonsynchronous Techniques; and Minneapolis-Honeywell's AVOIDS, for Avionic Observation of Intruder Danger System. All three of these were classified as "independent" systems, meaning that they were independent of ground control, since they were carried in the airplane itself.

All three systems were tested by the FAA, and in 1976 the agency announced that Honeywell's AVOIDS was the most satisfactory. But this did not mean acceptance, for the FAA had another concept in mind, one that it had sponsored and in part developed and that it felt was more compatible with the air traffic control system in use: a ground-based system.

There are, of course, two ways of going at the collision avoidance problem. One is with a "black box" carried in the airplane, which is able to sense, or "see," intruder airplanes ahead, behind, above, below, or on either side of the airplane. But beyond that, it must also tell the pilot what to do to avoid a collision, since there are only split-seconds in which to act, and a wrong maneuver could be disastrous. The second possibility is based on observers on the ground, who oversee a wide area of sky above with precision radar and who have computers on hand to give them instant warning when two aircraft are seen to be on a collision course. In this case, the pilot is alerted and given instructions at the same time: "Intruder at twelve o'clock. *Dive!*" or some such message.

There are advantages and disadvantages either way. The airborne system (ACAS, for Airborne Collision Avoidance System) might be faster in giving an alert, but less dependable in ordering evasive action; the ground-based concept (BCAS, with the *B* standing for "beacon") might be a hair slower but overall more reliable. The FAA made its decision on a different basis: it ultimately rejected AVOIDS because it was felt that a ground-based system was more compatible, and less likely to interfere, with the air traffic control system.

Undoubtedly, behind the decision also lay a few tattered shreds of the old concept of "freedom of the skies," which the FAA had been battling for so long. A pilot flying with an airborne black box was free to act as the black box told him to act. This was at odds with the basic concept of "positive control" by ground stations, which was the heart of the air traffic control system. Being human, a pilot would immediately climb if his ACAS told him to climb; he would get clearance for an altitude change later, when the danger of a collision had passed. But such actions could cause considerable confusion in the air traffic system and might even bring on the danger of other collisions.

A ground-based system, on the other hand, would be integrated with the air traffic control system, since it would depend upon a communications link between a ground station and the aircraft. To the FAA this was the deciding point, and in 1976 it committed itself firmly to the concept of a ground-based collision avoidance system.

As time and experiments went on, it became more and more

The avionics technician performs an increasingly important service to air safety.

apparent that the greatest problems lay in the area of greatest danger: at the airport, when an airplane took off or came in to land. An airborne system, for example, which might have been extremely effective in preventing the Grand Canyon collision, stuttered helplessly in a confusion of false alarms when tested in the heavy traffic of an airport situation. There was also serious interference with its signals, and the evasive maneuvers it could call for were so restricted that the system was in constant conflict with air traffic controllers.

The problem is also complicated by the fact that an effective anticollision system must provide not only collision alerts but also resolutions of these. Again, there is no time for neck craning and searching on the part of the pilot: he must be told what to do *now*. This is accomplished by a computer that has been programmed to interpret information on altitude, course, and speed, which it receives from both the protected aircraft and from the intruder plane, so that it can resolve the conflict with an order to the pilots. Here again, the airborne black box is at a disadvantage in a high-density-airport situation because there are just too many signal distractions.

Where do the signals from the intruder aircraft come from? Obviously, they cannot be simply radar return pulse signals which tell nothing of altitude, speed, or course. Out of the many studies pursued on this subject has emerged that extremely useful instrument, the transponder, which supplies identification, altitude, and airspeed for the data block on the radar sets of ground controllers. Following concept of the collision avoidance system that has survived all of the FAA tests, the transponder supplies this same information to the computer, with the course added, and the computer then works out the resolution of the conflict and sends it instantly to the pilot.

There is one drawback, apparently an unavoidable one: both aircraft must have encoding transponders, i.e., transponders that can provide the necessary information. What this will mean to the small, less well-heeled airplanes of the general aviation fleet must await introduction of the system, at which time further restrictions to flying in the immediate vicinity of major airports may well come under discussion.

A preliminary step toward collision avoidance—or separation assurance, as the FAA prefers to call it—is already in operation on some of the nation's airways and terminal areas. This is the Collision Alert in which a flashing data block warns the air traffic controller that one of his airplanes is heading into trouble. Along the airways, in the en route phase of flight, the Collision Alert signal allows two minutes to get the airplane out of danger; in the high-density area around an airport, only 40 seconds are provided.

The conflict alert and the fact that it is already operational is a good example of the FAA's philosophy on the Collision Avoidance System and how it will eventually be developed. As noted, the agency has long been on record as believing that no single black box will ever be the solution, but that it will be a combination, an integration, of systems that will eventually provide the answer. The Collision Alert is just such a system: it is a step along the road toward Conflict Alert and Resolution—in other words, something that will sound the alarm, then tell the pilot what to do to resolve the impending conflict.

Another component is something called Discrete Address Beacon System (DABS). The miraculous thing about DABS is that it can pick one single aircraft out of the clutter flying around an airport and talk to that aircraft specifically, giving it instructions to get through traffic, or warning it of an impending conflict situation, or whatever. Until now, communications between ground controllers and airplanes has always been subject to "garble," when not only radio transmission but the blips on the radar screen tend to overlap and become unintelligible.

The Collision Avoidance System, when it has finally been certificated by the FAA and introduced to the nation's airways and airports, will certainly have DABS as one of its components, just as the Conflict Alert System will be another.

Still another may be something called SMAW, for Safe Minimum Altitude Warning, which is already operational in some parts of the country. On February 20, 1981, SMAW covered itself with glory when it sounded an alarm warning that an Argentine airliner coming into Kennedy Airport was seconds away from a collision with the twin towers of The World Trade Center in downtown Manhattan. The nearest thing to so disastrous an event was the crash in 1944 of a B-25 Mitchell bomber into the Empire State Building in New York. But the Mitchell, a medium bomber, was far smaller than the four-engine Boeing 707 jet flown by the Argentine pilot, and the death of the 49 people on board the airliner—to say nothing of the carnage that it might well have wrought on the streets below—would have far outweighed the casualties in the Empire State Building crash.

There are rules, regulations, and specific headings for airliners to follow when they approach Kennedy Airport by flying across Manhattan, but, of course, things like this can always happen for unforeseen reasons. In this case the ground controller monitoring the Argentine plane suddenly noticed from the data block that the plane was 1,500 feet below its assigned altitude. At the same time, SMAW recognized that the plane was low and that it was only four miles from the World Trade Center, and so the device sounded its buzzer and flashed the data block. The controller, Donald Zimmerman, called the pilot and in urgent tones ordered him to climb to 3,000 feet and turn sharply to the south.

Another new system which will doubtless be integrated into the Collision Avoidance System is ATARS (Automatic Traffic Advisory and Resolution Service). Combined with DABS, this provides an instantaneous communications link over which certain aircraft can be ordered to do certain things to facilitate traffic movement and to avoid conflict. Furthermore, ATARS provides a service for both IFR and VFR traffic, which means that the movements of small aircraft in the airport area can also be followed and controlled.

Another development, long overdue, will eliminate the possibility of such horrible disasters as the runway collision between two Boeing 747 jumbo jets at Tenerife in the Canary Islands. That 1977 collision—one of the planes was taking off, the other had just landed—killed more than 570 people, by far the greatest number ever killed in an airplane accident anywhere. The reason for it was absurdly simple: the pilot taking off thought he heard the controller say "Okay," and he took it to mean "Okay for takeoff." The controller, however, had used it in an entirely different context and was horrified when he saw the big plane begin to roll and gather speed.

So today there is Visual Confirmation of Voice Takeoff Clearance (VICON). When a controller has cleared an airplane for takeoff, the pilot cannot begin his takeoff roll until he sees clusters of pulsing green lights along the runway's edge. This system also makes it possible to stop an airplane that has begun its takeoff on a false takeoff clearance.

Somebody at FAA finally came up with an unpronounceable acronym, LLWSAS, when a very important safety device called Low Level Wind Shear Alert System was developed. Wind shear is a phenomenon that can drop a landing airplane into the ground as though a huge hand were pushing it down. It can occur before or during a thunderstorm, or when a rapidly moving weather front approaches the airport and causes sudden shifts in wind force and direction. Its effect may be to cancel a headwind that suddenly reduces the air speed from 160 miles per hour to 60 and causes the airplane to stop flying and fall.

The wind shear device, as it is being developed at present, would sound an alarm in the control tower in the event of a sudden change in wind force and direction. The controller would then alert the pilot, who would add the weight of his own judgment and make a decision whether to add power, thereby increasing his airspeed to cancel out the effect of the wind, or whether to abort the landing.

All these systems, and more, have been developed either by the FAA itself or by private industry in response to FAA suggestions. In either event, they are tested and evaluated by the FAA before they are accepted and certificated for use on the nation's airways. The place where this is done is a gleaming white building alongside an airfield on the outskirts of Atlantic City, New Jersey. This is the National Aviation Facilities Experimental Center (NAFEC). The airfield has a 10,000-foot runway, big enough to accommodate the largest of jumbo jets. There are, in addition, numberless fascinating gadgets standing around: a mock-up of a fuselage, which is used to perfect equipment and techniques for protecting passengers in an airplane that catches fire after crashing; a mast that can emit horizontal plumes of varicolored smoke, which is used to study the vortex effects of airplanes and decide on steps to protect other aircraft from the resulting turbulence; and, of course, all kinds of radar equipment, which may or may not find its way into the collision avoidance or air traffic control programs.

In time, and as money becomes available, many of these devices will spread from the large airports for which they are now primarily intended to the smaller satellite airports, which have already begun to absorb much of the nation's general aviation traffic. Orange County Airport near Los Angeles is one example of this; Teterboro Airport, across the George Washington Bridge from Manhattan, is another. Both are easily reachable by bus, helicopter, or automobile from the big cities they serve and both enjoy all the safety benefits of ground-controlled traffic regulation.

Of course, aviation has lost much of its old-time freedom and charm as it has grown to its present formidable size. But ours is a crowded planet on which we must all survive. Those who died in the Cutter Crash or whose last sight of the earth was the whirling mosaic of the Grand Canyon as they spun down from 21,000 feet will never again know what it is like to make a safe landing at the airport of their choice, as millions do today.

Twenty years ago I used to fly down from the Connecticut skies onto Danbury Airport, a few miles from where I live. Sometimes the setting sun was full in my eyes as I glided, 100 feet above a hillside, toward the runway. Sometimes the sky was gray and the runway white with snow. But, always, I felt the runway welcoming me, giving me happiness to be back home.

Danbury Airport is still there. But where Piper Cubs used to frolic there are now stern, shiny corporate jets, gleaming twin-engine Beechcraft, Cessnas, and Navajos—a whole new generation of planes. Some of them even fly right to the coastline and across the ocean to distant lands overseas.

And there is also a control tower. I recently flew out of Danbury at night with my son, and as we poised at the end of the runway, where I had so often made my own takeoff clearance many years ago, I heard the controller's voice: "Piper 9013-Delta, cleared for takeoff." And when we returned and announced ourselves to the tower, there was the same calm, quiet voice clearing us to land.

To me, it again seemed like a welcome, this time from a protecting voice on the ground. I like it better that way.

Chapter 11
Aviation Weather

The sky above us is an ocean of air. Like the ocean, it offers limitless possibilities for transportation and adventure, but like the ocean it also harbors many invisible dangers and risks. The sky, so peaceful, so transparent, has currents and eddies, storms of wind and rain, snow and ice, towering waves, and great masses of trackless cloud in which an airplane can go as perilously astray as any vessel groping its way along a fogbound coast. To a pilot it is as essential to know the vagaries of the sky as it is for a seaman to know his ocean.

To aviation, weather is the most important aspect of the sky. It constantly threatens to limit operations, and it is the one factor in flying that took the longest to fathom and to overcome. When Charles Lindbergh crossed the Atlantic to Paris in 1927, flying was still in the "seat of the pants" stage: with only primitive instruments to guide them, Lindbergh and his peers had to fly by instinct, trusting that their own sense of balance, aided by altimeter, turn-and-bank indicator, and compass, would keep their airplanes right side up and flying where they wanted to go. Sometimes it worked; sometimes, tragically, it did not, for without a visible horizon one's sense of balance quickly becomes totally confused.

A crucial difference between the sailor's and the pilot's view of weather is the simple fact that for the aviator it is a matter of immediate concern. Whatever is going on up ahead where those clouds loom so threateningly, he is approaching it at anywhere from 115 to 550 miles per hour, depending on the type of airplane he is flying. There is little time to look things up, think things over, shorten sail, and batten down the hatches. Something is going to happen—very soon.

A number of years ago I was flying the Atlantic with Max Conrad, probably the greatest long-distance pilot the world has ever known. We had been flying at 9,000 feet for perhaps ten hours (out of Boston) in very stable air beneath a high ceiling of feathery cirrus clouds. It was growing dark, and out of the darkness in the eastern sky ahead of us, a great cloud mass loomed, stretching to either side as far as the eye could see.

Max eyed it speculatively. "If we knew how high it was, we might be able to top it. But I hate to use a lot of gas climbing and then find out we did it all for nothing."

Just then the radio crackled. It was a MATS transport plane answering a question put by a Pan Am airliner coming up behind us. "I'm at 16,000 feet and I'm still in it," he said.

"Well," said Max. "Now, we know. Hang on; it'll be bumpy for a while."

A few minutes later the cloud mass was directly ahead. It was like flying into a mountainside. In a fraction of a second the world disappeared. A loud hissing sound enveloped us, Max shouted: "Watch!" and touched a finger to the windshield. A long blue spark of static electricity suddenly appeared at his fingertip, and now I saw the nose of the airplane was glowing eerily. "Saint Elmo's fire," Max shouted. He was enjoying it enormously.

This little incident is cited to show how quickly weather phenomena can affect aircraft. If we had been flying through smooth skies before, we were now, as far as the weather was concerned, at precisely the opposite extreme. The sky was an unforgettable panorama of towering clouds, rising far higher than our own 9,000 feet of altitude, and in between these immense pillars of darkness the air was as rough as a storm at sea. And this change had come about literally in the blink of an eye!

How did the early fliers learn to deal with these eccentricities of the new medium into which they were venturing? By trial and error. There was no other way. There were no voices in the sky to warn them, no forecasts on the ground to tell them what they might encounter. Lindbergh in his book, *The Spirit of St. Louis*, described how he encountered icing over the ocean on his way to Paris: he had no alternative but to descend, even if it meant getting perilously close to the water, until the ice melted away.

When Max Conrad took me through the formalities of clearing Customs and otherwise checking out of Boston's Logan Airport, he got a weather briefing, complete with detailed map, from the Weather office. How have such things come about in modern times?

Like so many developments in American aviation, weather briefing was long in coming. It had its origins in 1812, when the first private ventures in weather reporting and forecasting were made. But these were so primitive and local in nature that they were scarcely of any importance. By 1849 Joseph Henry, the secretary of the Smithsonian Institution, brought a scientific mind and scientific methods to bear on the problem. He realized that the only reliable method of reporting and predicting the weather was with the help of reporting stations located in many places, a network that would make possible the drawing of a weather map. And twenty years later, in 1869, Cleveland Abbe, the director of the Cincinnati Observatory, established a meteorological network that covered a useful amount of territory and showed that a systematic weather service was not only a possibility but would be of widespread benefit as well.

In 1870 Congress in a joint resolution voted for the establishment of a weather service, with particular attention paid to providing warnings for ships at sea and communities on land in the Great Lakes area and along the seacoasts. The United States Army Signal Corps was appointed to establish and carry out this service, which it did for twenty years, until, in 1891, the Weather Bureau was created in the Department of Agriculture. It took until 1918 to initiate daily weather forecasts, which were begun at that time to facilitate the operation of the first airmail service.

These, as we now know, were the doldrum years for aviation in the United States, the years of barnstorming and flying circuses, when no one could yet see sufficient profits in flying to attempt seriously to develop it. Not until the Kelly Act of 1925 and the Air Commerce Act of 1926 put airmail on a firm foundation was an attempt made to develop the meteorological service in a manner that would make it really useful to pilots, like Lindbergh, who daily risked their lives to carry the mail. The first efforts to map winds aloft were undertaken, using kites to carry instruments into the upper air.

By 1938, when air travel was a lusty, booming business in the country, the number of daily forecasts was increased from two to four, partly in answer to the devastation wrought by the terrible hurricane that swept New England entirely without warning that year. Two years later, in wartime, the Weather Bureau was transferred to the Department of Commerce.

The weather briefing Max Conrad and I received in February, 1959, was the result of a system that incorporated 244 Weather Bureau officers and airport stations throughout the United States, fixed ocean stations in the Atlantic and Pacific, and 5 stations in the Arctic. This meteorological network, furthermore, was tied in with an international network of reporting stations which spanned the entire globe. With the advent, in the next few years, of weather satellites the art of weather reporting and prediction would finally advance to something approaching an exact science, and aviation would benefit accordingly.

What is this ocean of air that now demands—and gets—such close attention?

It is unique to our solar system—a blanket of mixed gases which are capable of sustaining life. Nitrogen makes up more than three-quarters of it; oxygen makes up somewhat less than a quarter; and a mixture of argon, carbon dioxide, helium, and other gases makes up the rest. Water vapor is always present in it to some degree. And this blanket of air, by its very nature, is always in motion.

The blanket of air surrounding the earth is called the atmosphere, and within it we distinguish several layers. Only two of these concern aviation: the troposphere, which extends from 55,000 to 65,000 feet above the surface of the earth; and the stratosphere, which extends from the top of the troposphere up to from 26 to 29 miles above the earth's surface.

Some years ago, when transport airplanes were first equipped pressurized cabins and the ability to cruise at high altitudes, press agents for the airlines, with their usual license, advertised: "Fly in comfort, over the weather, high in the stratosphere!" What was true about this statement was that airplanes flying over 25,000 feet are, for the most part, flying over the weather, but they are not flying in the stratosphere. The troposphere is where most of the weather occurs, and lying above it does make for smoother flying. But passenger planes do not normally fly at such high altitudes that they are in the stratosphere, nor do they need to. If they wish to avoid weather, they can do so by flying in the upper troposphere or in the tropopause, a narrow band that marks the boundary between the troposphere and the stratosphere.

Since it is weather that concerns us here, let us examine how weather originates in the first place. One of the factors that stimulates a change in the weather is temperature. We know as a rule of thumb that the temperature goes down the higher we rise above the earth's surface: it is always colder at the top of a mountain than it is at sea level. However, there are exceptions to this rule. These exceptions are among the factors that generate weather, and for the safety of their passengers, airplane pilots should know about them.

Land and water absorb temperature in different degrees. Water absorbs it rapidly, and thus a river, lake, or even a pond may contribute in some part to the generation of weather. Pilots learned long ago that if their approach to an airport led them above plowed fields and then over a lake, they should keep their approach high just before the airport runway since they could expect the airplane to sink noticeably once they were over the water. Heat reflected from the plowed fields, on the other hand, would cause the airplane to rise: this is the sort of rising column of air, called a thermal, that soaring pilots seek when they are out in their sailplanes.

There are also times when temperature does not decrease with altitude, but *increases*, often in association with a layer of cloud. This causes a temperature inversion, a very important weather phenomenon. For one thing, an inversion traps the layers of air below it, preventing air close to the ground from rising. Los Angeles is noted for such temperature inversions, which have made it one of the most smog-plagued cities of the world. Another city with very bad smog problems is Milan, Italy. In this case a so-called ground inversion is the culprit: the air around Milan's surrounding marshlands cools off more quickly than the warm air above does, and thus the surface air stops rising as it normally would. Fog is generated and, as so often happens in the autumn, Milan's two airports are then closed.

A temperature inversion may also occur during a weather change, for example when an incoming warm front overrides cold air near the ground. In this case, rain falling aloft may turn to ice when it encounters the cold air nearer the ground, and a pilot runs into an entirely unanticipated problem.

Air is in virtually constant motion; therefore, the atmosphere around us is in constant change. There are global winds, the tradewinds, for example, which arise as a result of the Coriolis effect, which is caused by the spin of the globe; there are winds that circulate between areas of high and low pressure, or between areas of high and low temperature; there are valley and mountain winds which may occur as regularly as clockwork at sunrise or sunset because of temperature variations. All these affect aircraft to a

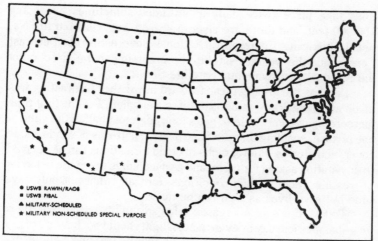

Synoptic upper air observation sites

greater or lesser degree. Even such an extremely local phenomenon as a dust devil, a rapidly spinning column of rising warm air, can toss a light aircraft about, sometimes to a dangerous degree.

The prediction of winds aloft is of great importance to any pilot planning a long distance flight and is, of course, crucially important to airlines for the maintenance of their schedules. But it is only since World War II that winds aloft and many other weather phenomena could be charted and predicted with any real degree of accuracy. One development was the balloon-borne radiosonde, a small package containing a radio transmitter and sensitive instruments for measuring temperature, barometric pressure, and other pertinent data. Not only could the speed and direction of the balloon's flight at various altitudes be measured, but atmospheric conditions could be charted and correlated so that a body of knowledge about conditions in the upper atmosphere could be built up.

The FAA, for its part, impressed upon pilots the importance of giving Pilot's Reports (PIREPs) about conditions as they flew along. Pilots know best what is important to pilots, and these reports are among the most valuable items in the body of meteorological information built up daily about conditions in the air.

The weather service available to pilots is the result of a collaborative effort between the National Weather Service and the Federal Aviation Administration. There is also input from the military weather services and from foreign weather services, which contribute to the global nature of the operation. Upper air observations take place twice daily at altitudes sometimes exceeding 100,000 feet, and there are also, in season, reports from the National Hurricane Center, the National Severe Storms Forecast Center, and the weather satellite program, under the direction of the National Environmental Satellite Service.

Perhaps the greatest leap forward in weather forecasting was made when the first weather satellites went aloft. For the first time meteorologists were able to get a look at almost half of the wind in one picture, enabling them to trace precise patterns of winds, cloud cover, and storms. Photographs of cloud formations can be relayed to any station asking for them, and as data builds up on the behavior of weather under certain conditions, forecasts that not only save time but save lives as well can be made.

Today, there is no reason why any pilot setting out on a long-distance journey or even a short flight should not have all of the latest weather reports beforehand, so that he can make all necessary plans to have a safe trip. The service is available free of charge and he can either seek it out in person by stopping in at a Flight Service Station (FSS) or weather office, or call up and get it over the telephone.

The FSS is his most likely choice and also the one that provides him with the most information. From this source the pilot can get a preflight briefing which he can continually update as his flight progresses. The FSS also makes regular weather broadcasts and, in times of unsettled weather, unscheduled broadcasts and weather advisories.

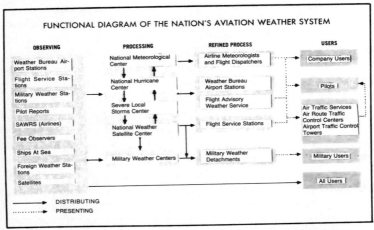

Collection and dissemination of aviation weather data in the United States.

The weather radar network.

In addition, certain stations also provide taped weather broadcasts (TWEBs) which run continually on low to medium radio frequencies and on the navigational Omni ranges (VORs). The PATWAS (Pilot's Automatic Telephone Weather Answering Service) gives the same information automatically by phone.

All weather broadcasts follow a set order which is also the key to reading the teletype weather service available at most airports. These may at first seem impenetrable to the noninitiate (MDW RS 1856-X M7 0VC 11/2R+F 990 /63/61/3205/980/RF2 RB12), but as one becomes accustomed to the sequence and code, reading a weather report becomes routine.

An additional safety feature of the FAA's weather report service is the recommendation of alternate routes to pilots facing hazardous weather. Flight Watch, as the enroute service is called, also gives quick recognition and dissemination to the weather reports of other pilots on the route (PIREPs). There are now 44 Flight Service Stations in operation, covering the country from Maine to California, and the service can be had at anytime by calling Flight Watch on 122.0 MHz.

Headwinds, fog, ice, heavy rain—all these are hazards to the pilot, but probably the most feared of all dangers aloft is the thunderstorm. A thunderstorm is elemental violence let loose, a concentration of power such as one may encounter nowhere else except in a hurricane or tornado. Rain, wind, ice, lightning—a thunderstorm has all these, plus updrafts and downdrafts of such violence that they can tear an airplane apart.

The danger of a thunderstorm is usually—although not always—heralded by a towering cumulus cloud. This is because every thunderstorm starts out as such a cloud; i.e., in its initial stage it is a strong updraft that draws condensation with it as it rises, thus increasing the size of the cumulus cloud. Some pilots have tried to climb over the tops of cumulus clouds growing in this manner only to find they rise higher faster than their airplane can climb—3,000 feet per minute or more.

An icing hazard enters the picture when the upward-borne raindrops reach the freezing level. At this point, they begin to fall as heavy drops of rain, creating a downdraft within the cloud. An airplane flying into this may very well be stressed beyond the breaking point since the windshear forces between updrafts and downdrafts are enormous.

This is the second, or mature stage of the thunderstorm. The cold air rushing downward may travel more than 2,500 feet per

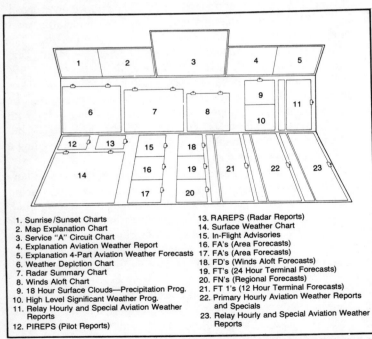

1. Sunrise/Sunset Charts
2. Map Explanation Chart
3. Service "A" Circuit Chart
4. Explanation Aviation Weather Report
5. Explanation 4-Part Aviation Weather Forecasts
6. Weather Depiction Chart
7. Radar Summary Chart
8. Winds Aloft Chart
9. 18 Hour Surface Clouds—Precipitation Prog.
10. High Level Significant Weather Prog.
11. Relay Hourly and Special Aviation Weather Reports
12. PIREPS (Pilot Reports)
13. RAREPS (Radar Reports)
14. Surface Weather Chart
15. In-Flight Advisories
16. FA's (Area Forecasts)
17. FA's (Area Forecasts)
18. FD's (Winds Aloft Forecasts)
19. FT's (24 Hour Terminal Forecasts)
20. FN's (Regional Forecasts)
21. FT 1's (12 Hour Terminal Forecasts)
22. Primary Hourly Aviation Weather Reports and Specials
23. Relay Hourly and Special Aviation Weather Reports

The Weather Bureau Airport Station (WBAS) display, received by Teletype, is often available at airports without a weather office or Flight Service Station.

minute, and at the bottom of the cloud, the downdraft becomes a torrent of wind that brings with it a sharp drop in temperature. The updrafts in the meantime may have reached twice their earlier speed, traveling at more than 6,000 feet per minute. The mature stage is the most violent stage of the storm, with strong, gusty winds, lightning, and sheets of rain at ground level.

We have seen that thunderstorms are almost always surrounded by towering cumulus clouds; the *almost* refers to the fact that sometimes a storm may be hidden in a bank of heavy cloud. Weather-avoidance radar will detect it, but it is otherwise invisible. For this reason, if the weather service reports thunderstorms in the area, pilots who do not have radar fly around such banks of heavy cloud.

Under no circumstances should a pilot attempt to fly underneath a storm. It may look harmless enough, with only rain showing, but the turbulence under a thunderstorm is explosive, with air rushing in to feed the updraft and the strong wind of the downdraft rushing out.

There was a time, not so long ago, when pilots—even airline pilots—had few defenses against thunderstorms beyond their own

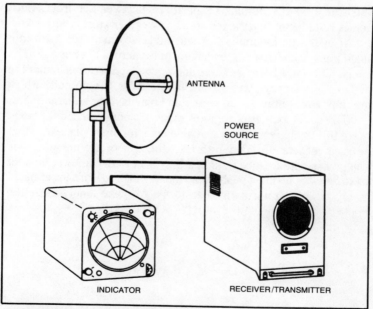

Airborne weather radar is now found in many general aviation aircraft as well as in all airliners.

eyes and their own skills and experience. In a memorable literary passage in *Fate Is the Hunter*, Ernest K. Gann describes how as a young copilot he was trained in evading and, if necessary, flying through thunderstorms in upstate New York, a notable breeder of storms. And an Air Force pilot who lived to tell the tale once recounted his hair-raising adventure when, forced to bail out of his fighter plane in a thunderstorm, he found himself carried *up* thousands of feet in his parachute, only to be hurled downward again when the downdraft caught him. He was finally spewed out, more dead than alive and with his clothing frozen stiff.

Tornados are very localized storms that grow from thunderstorms. The birth of a tornado occurs when the air drawn into the base of the cumulus cloud is given a spinning motion. This sets up a very concentrated vortex that appears to the eye as a twisting, funnel-shaped cloud reaching into the base of the storm itself. If the tip of the funnel touches the earth, it has sufficient power to uproot trees, tear houses apart, and toss heavy trucks and freight cars about like matchboxes. The wind may be spinning at well over 200 miles per hour, and a tornado is one of the most fearful forces in nature.

Usually tornados are formed by "steady-state" thunderstorms, which may be the heralds of an advancing weather front. Such storms last longer than the isolated hot-weather storms with which almost everyone is familiar. Steady-state storms often form into squall lines, which may extend many miles across the horizon. The crucial difference between them and the isolated storms is that the rainfall, in a steady-state storm, falls *outside* the updraft, which therefore can continue unhindered and may last for several hours.

The development of weather radar has now reached the point where this equipment is not available even for small planes, so that the greatest fear of thunderstorms—the fear of the unknown—is largely dissipated. Since their anatomy is now also known, no pilot has to feel that he must push ahead into a storm to learn for himself. Enough is known about thunderstorms to make amply clear the simplest of all rules: "Stay away!"

Chapter 12
Flight by Acronym

It is ironic that American air traffic controllers decided to go on strike in the spring of 1981, a time when their further contribution to safety in the air was being questioned as never before. Since the days of the little room in Cleveland in which the first air traffic controllers fought with and solved the intricacies of the system they had to create out of nothing, human control of airplanes aloft by people on the ground had been taken for granted. "We have come to appreciate the truly remarkable capability of human controllers to manage terminal air traffic and to achieve efficient airport operations," said Siegbert B. Poritzky of the FAA in a speech to the Airport Operators Council International in Mexico City in October, 1980. "[It] may be extremely difficult to duplicate [these capacities] with automation." Yet automation was waiting just around the corner, and when members of the Professional Air Traffic Controllers Organization (PATCO) went on strike, they walked right into an automated trap.

Not that there was anything deliberate about this; nobody planned it that way. But one might suppose that, in the years since the dawn of the Jet Age, as airplanes flew ever higher, faster, and further and carried more people, automation would creep up on the air traffic control system. The complaints over which the PATCO members went on strike—bad working conditions, too much stress on the job, obsolete equipment, to name a few—had been valid for years. President Ronald Reagan—the man who fired the controllers when they struck—himself acknowledged as much when he promised, during his election campaign, to take care of these grievances once he was elected president, whereupon the members of PATCO turned out enthusiastically to vote for him. But whether President Reagan could or would have done any more for the flight controllers than any other president before him must remain a matter of conjecture.

The truth of the matter is that the growth of aviation from the time of the Wright brothers' first flight has been so frenetic and has dragged so many complexities in its wake that human effort has been hard put to keep up with it. After all, *the whole business, from Kitty Hawk to the Boeing 747 and the Space Shuttle, has grown up in barely the space of a lifetime!* That means that there are people alive today who can remember a world without airplanes and all the hideous complexities that these have brought with them. An example is the problem of air traffic control.

Perhaps this is one area that computers *can* handle better than human beings are capable of doing. Computers can detect instantly when two airplanes are likely to crash and cause them to diverge with plenty of time to spare. An *exceptional* controller in New York was able to detect when an airplane was flying in such a way that it would hit The World Trade Center; he gave an instant change of course with which the pilot instantly complied, and disaster was averted. But if that controller had been less alert, and if the pilot of the plane had said "What?" or "Why?" instead of immediately turning his plane, there would have been an unimaginable disaster.

Computers don't get tired, or sleepy, or bored. Computers don't respond to orders with a question. Computers don't get scared, and they don't get overstressed when airplanes start arriving all at once, like a flock of migrant birds.

This is not to say that computers are the answer or that they have the answer. But let us take a look at what they *might* do.

In a lovely country setting of rolling fields, woods, rivers, and bays near Hampton, Virginia, lies the NASA Langley Research Center where the National Aeronautics and Space Administration conducts most of its research into advanced problems of flying and space travel. Langley Center is an impressive complex of laboratories, wind tunnels, runways and simulators, but one of the most impressive pieces of equipment on it is what appears to be a used airplane—"used" in the sense that it has been around for some time—a twin-engine, chubby Boeing 737 jet that is normally used for medium- to short-haul flights in the passenger trade.

One look inside the 737 will show that it is far from being what it seems. Step in the door, turn your head to the left: there is the flight deck with all its innumerable dials and switches, its view out of the windshield at the runway ahead. Turn your head to the right: there is what appears to be the nose of another Boeing 737, sitting right in the middle of the passenger compartment!

It looks almost as though two airplanes had been telescoped into each other in some bizarre rear-end crash. Except that this intruder could not be a 737; it is too small. It fits into the cabin space with a little room left to walk around it and look at all the other equipment stowed away: rows and rows of electronic machinery, with dials and lights and trailing wires like some of the special effects in "Star Trek."

What we are looking at here actually *is* two planes in one. If we look inside the intruding airplane's front end, we see another flight deck, just like the real one we saw a moment ago on entering. Dials, switches, and controls are all there. But ah! There is something different. The windows are blind, as though obscured by a heavy fog. And below, on the instrument panel, is an array of panels that look like television screens.

They are, in fact, cathode ray tubes—the same type of electronic equipment that makes a television screen or a radar display. On the ground, air traffic controllers watch cathode ray tubes (CRTs) as the sweeping finger of light goes around and around, outlining airplanes in the sky with each sweep. Superimposed on CRTs like these can be visual guideposts of all kinds: the patterns of runways, for example, or visual reference points like islands, rivers, and tall buildings. Cathode ray tubes can be very magical things.

But none more magical than these in the simulated flight deck of Langley Research Center's Boeing 737. For these can be used to precisely locate the 737 in the empty void of sky, and they can be used to fly this same airplane from Langley to whatever airport is its destination with great precision and to land it on the runway of that airport even if the runway, the airport, the sky, and the world outside are totally obscured by clouds.

Not only can this be done, it *has* been done, over and over again in the last few years, by a pilot sitting, isolated from the outside world, in this inside flight deck of the Boeing 737. He sees absolutely nothing except what is inside this flight deck since he has no windows to the outside. But *he* flies the plane—"flying by wire," as the pilots call it when they fly by instruments in bad weather.

Some 20 years ago I was flying on one of my first solo cross-country trips, from Danbury, Connecticut, to Albany, New York. It was a brilliantly clear day in early summer. No clouds obscured the azure sky. No haze smudged the landscape below me. I could see with total clarity from horizon to horizon. And yet, as I came up the Hudson River toward Albany, I got lost some 15 or 20 miles out from the airport.

It was not a singular experience; it can happen to any pilot, some of them far more experienced than I was on that summer day long ago. I was not alarmed—I had a good map beside me, plenty of gas, and, above all, the blessing of that flawless day. But as I tried to orient myself, shifting my studious gaze from the map to the ground and back to the map and back to the ground again, I grew more and more frustrated, indignant, and, finally, just plain mad. That a person with normal intelligence and at least rudimentary training should be unable to find a place as big as a whole airport on a day like this . . . It seemed beyond the powers of rational belief.

Let me now superimpose this situation into the interior flight deck—or Aft Flight Deck (AFD), as it is called—of the NASA 737 at Langley and attempt to explain what those magical CRTs can do:

I am not staring out of the window, trying to locate Albany on the ground, but staring at a television screen conveniently located at eyeball height on the instrument panel in front of me. It has some strange-looking lines and bars on it—reference points lined up with the horizon outside to help me keep the airplane flying straight and level. If I should tilt, a bar will tilt until I correct with the controls and straighten the airplane again. Similarly, it shows me if I am dropping or raising the nose, in which case the "horizon" will drop or rise too.

Basically, this is the kind of display that any pilot would like to have—and many do—for instrument flying. But this is more, much more: it is an Electronic Attitude Director Indicator (EADI). It has built into it the kind of information that I can normally only get by letting my eyes scan constantly across all those dials on the instrument panel: air speed, altitude, rate of climb or rate of sink, power output, and so on. Furthermore, when I do finally find Albany and make my approach to the airport, flying by instruments, of course, in this totally blanked-out flight deck, I will see, as I draw near the runway, a television picture suddenly fill the lower half of the screen. There it will be, the runway, flight's end, safety, mother's arms, beautifully projected for me by a Low Level television camera housed in the nose of the airplane, just where I need it.

But that is for later, when I have found Albany. For the moment, I am still flying around in the skies above the Hudson, trying to locate myself—which is, as I remarked before, one of the most important, baffling, and trying jobs a pilot has to perform, anywhere, anytime.

It is a cliché to say that the sky is an awfully big place. It beats even the sea for size, and furthermore it is three dimensional. It is sometimes extraordinarily difficult to locate other objects in it and even more difficult to find out where they are going and at what speed. Another airplane a thousand feet below looks like a toy until, suddenly, one realizes that it is a thousand feet below and *climbing*. At that point it looks as big and solid as a battleship and the matter of where is it climbing to become an urgent concern.

Enter now another CRT smiling up at me from the instrument panel. This one is labeled with the letters "EHSI," standing for Electronic Horizontal Situation Indicator. This is the heavyweight part of the computerized system, the one that does things that have never been done before—like telling a pilot *exactly* where he is with respect to where he ought to be.

Albany lies on a river, as big and beautiful and generally visible a river as you are likely to find anywhere. Twenty years ago I looked down on this river, saw an airport, and thought: "Aha! Gotcha!" And promptly called Albany to announce my presence, directly above.

Albany looked out the window. But I wasn't there.

Well, there is no point in reliving the confusion, embarrassment and chagrin of that early initiation into the complexities of aerial navigation. I finally realized that I had "found" the wrong airport—that I was circling Schenectady, while Albany lay elsewhere, even though it was not very far away as the airplane flies. But had I tried then to imagine the kind of ideal navigational tool I wanted to fly with, I would have come up with something very like the EHSI. I wanted very much to have my situation indicated to me.

Which is exactly what the EHSI does. In the center of it is a little movable marker, like the signs that say "You Are Here." From the pointed front end of the marker of the EHSI extends a thin line that might aptly be tagged "You Will Be Here in 30 Seconds," because it shows you where you *are* going.

Elsewhere on the display is another thin line that shows you where you *should* be going. That line is the track of your scheduled flight route, which will have been prescribed by the FAA to give you the shortest distance between two points and also keep you clear of other airplanes. And on that line is a small box that shows where your airplane is supposed to be at this moment. When the pilot turns a small steering knob and gets his "You Are Here" marker into the box, he is *there*. All he has to do is to stay inside that box, which will move along the track even as the airplane moves across the countryside, until the EHSI tells him he has arrived at his destination. At that point it will tell him how to land the airplane.

In addition to these astonishing feats, the EHSI also displays information on altitude, ground speed, and how well the flight is keeping up with the flight plan. If I am scheduled to arrive at Albany at, say, 11:38 A.M., the EHSI may inform me that I am now 23 seconds late and, furthermore, that I am 19 feet above my prescribed altitude of 5,000 feet. That's not much of an error on a standards altimeter; in fact, it wouldn't show up at all. But this airplane uses a radio altimeter which bounces signals off the ground and thus gets instant and extremely accurate readings. Those 19 feet probably account for at least some of the 23 seconds I am late, since they indicate I am in a gentle climb, which I can now correct. All of this information, I might add, is digitally displayed where I can see it with scarcely any movement of my eyes.

This ease of eyeball movement is no accident, either; it is part of a studied plan to ease the stress put on pilots. There is at Langley a piece of equipment called an oculometer, the specific purpose of which is to chart the movements of a pilot's eyeballs as he scans his various instruments and navigational displays. I remember there was an article in *Life* magazine many years ago, which charted, via light bulbs on her feet, the many steps a housewife had to take in her kitchen while she was preparing dinner. The oculometer turns out similar charts of the many flicks and zips a pilot's eyeballs make as they move from airspeed indicator to altimeter to articial horizon to exhaust temperature and so on. It does this by means of a beam of infrared-sensitive light that is aimed at the pilot's pupils and deflected back from there to an infrared-sensitive television camera. The result is a chart of zigzag lines superimposed on the background of the instruments concerned.

What about the pilot? Does he go blind while all this is happening? Not at all. He sees only a dim red glow that doesn't bother him. But in time he may notice that his instruments have been regrouped and seem somehow easier to read.

The information that the EHSI displays in so matter-of-fact a fashion all comes to it automatically through computers. Altitude information, of course, is fairly direct: it comes from the radio altimeter. But it has the potential of being projected against other information—for example, against a range of mountains looming up ahead, or a tall television tower 25 miles away on the present course. If altitude must be changed to clear these hazards, a warning will be sounded and instructions will be displayed.

Time-speed-distance information comes from the computer being tuned in (automatically) on Distance Measuring Equipment (DME) beacons along the flight track down below. On the airways in the United States, DME beacons are being installed in increasing numbers to help the airplane keep track of its progress and location. Tie DMEs into computer systems such as those carried by NASA's 737 and almost anything is possible: "You are 23 seconds behind schedule, Pilot Knauth. You should increase your speed by so-and-so-much and adjust your trim tab to lose that 19 feet of altitude and attain level flight."

Marvels apart, what can this sort of equipment do for present-day air travel, aside from reducing the pilot to a state of thumb-twiddling boredom as he flies along?

One thing it can do is to knock most of the men who at present monitor and regulate the flight of aircraft on the nation's airways—the flight controllers—out of a job. Not today, not tomorrow, not next year—but some time within the next ten years. That is the FAA's own estimate and explains the calm with which they viewed the president's firing of most of their air controllers: they knew they weren't going to need them anyway. Over the next ten years, these men and women will gradually leave—attrition—and they won't be replaced.

The main reason for this is the EHSI, which tells a pilot firmly: "You are here." The "here" may be 210 nautical miles from his destination, on the 210-degree radial outbound of the next VOR navigational station, at 19,993 feet altitude and flying at 493 nautical miles per hour. At present a flight controller on the ground and the airplane's own instruments can give him more or less the same information but not with such accuracy and only after a good deal of sweat has been put into various computations, which a computer makes in the blink of an eye. And which way of keeping track of your flight would you, a passenger, prefer to see used?

What does it take to do all this? First of all, it takes a general-purpose computer to do the navigation work, one with a 32K memory and a 24-bit word size; then, as a primary input sensor, an inertial navigation system which, basically, keeps track of the airplane's movements (it does this in much the same way that an atomic submarine keeps track of its whereabouts in the black void of the world's oceans). Finally, it takes a complex and sensitive set of gyroscopes which have been precisely aligned with certain points of the compass before the flight begins. Once set up and set spinning, these gyroscopes can be used to measure movement in any direction with the aid of a very precise laser beam. The gyroscopes resist any movement that deviates from the axis of their spin, as a bicycle wheel held in both hands will resist efforts to turn it. This resistance can be measured with the laser beam, and computations that only a computer can make can calculate from those figures the direction of movement, the distance of the movement, and all the rest. To say it is precise is almost an understatement.

Both flight controllers and pilots have reason to fear the EHSI: it is a direct threat to their jobs. As far as pilots are concerned, it certainly undercuts their argument that three men are needed in the cockpit to run the airplane safely: On the other hand, it is to be hoped that if the airplane operators argue that one man in the cockpit is enough when EHSI is aboard, the pilots will stand firm: it does not seem likely that the flying public would like the idea of flying with only one human being and a computer between them and a frightful and painful end.

In other words, it is very easy to get carried away by the technological wonders of EHSI and EADI. It is great to sit comfortably at home and read about airplanes that land themselves without a pilot touching the controls, but it is different to buy a seat on such a plane and know that only transistors and wires stand between the plane's passengers and flaming death. Two men in the cockpit should be the absolute minimum.

Let us imagine now that the miracle of EHSI has brought us to the airport of our destination. This is where we use the Electronic Attitude Director Indicator we spoke of earlier. This is also an airport serviced by a microwave landing system, which surrounds the entire airport with an envelope of microwaves distributed in grid form like a fishnet thrown over the whole area. The microwave signals also play their part in steering the airplane to a safe landing.

When the proper buttons are pushed, the cathode ray display of the EADI comes alive. The flight reference symbols show up: the lines simulating the airplane, the horizon, the runway. The television picture appears, and it is precisely aligned with the symbols. The projected touchdown point shows up; the runway numbers appear and flash past; the airplane flares and floats, losing its airspeed; and still all the symbols are right where they should be on the runway. The tires touch down; the plane has landed. The reverse thrusters roar and the brakes take hold—all automatically. The airplane leaves the runway at the first available exit and trundles along the taxiway to the gate. The flight is over.

There is one more item to add to this picture, and this is the most controversial of all. If computers will be replacing flight controllers along the airways, what will happen in the terminal areas, where the traffic is most dense and the danger of collision between airplanes greatest? How do EHSI and EADI fit in with the Collision Avoidance System?

The answer is, they fit like a glove. Add a few more buttons, a few more sensors, and associated machinery and you have, to use NASA jargon, "CDTI interfacing into the EHSI" (translated as Cockpit Display of Traffic Information has been hooked into the Electronic Horizontal Situation indicator).

With this set-up, not only will the CRT show all the other things the pilot wants to know—like where he is and where he is going—but it will also show him all other aircraft that may be in the vicinity. This, of course, may be more than the pilot wants to know, but it is better to know and get out of the way than otherwise. And in a reasonably well regulated situation, the airplanes will be able to get out of each other's way, once the system is operative.

That time, of course, may be a long ways off. For the moment it can be said that NASA's Boeing 737, with its fully panoply of cockpit displays, including CDTI, in its first experiments made nearly 100 landings; it did so flying by wire in Category Three visibility (visibility zero) in a sky full of simulated airplanes, all of which showed up on the CDTI. It was like landing in a pea soup fog at Kennedy Airport in New York at the height of the rush hour. And every landing went off like clockwork.

Something like this will happen, although it is still a long way from Langley Research Center to the cockpits of the nation's airplanes. Any system that relies on computers will have to be extraordinarily safe, if only to assuage the fears of computer manufacturers who have nightmares in which one of their machines "goes down" and causes a crash that takes several hundred people with it. As matters stand, the FAA has a billion dollars and ten years set aside to introduce the new era of Flight by Acronym, or the Computerized Age. And in an ironic footnote to history, Ronald Reagan's firing of the air traffic controllers who served the country so long and so well was the first step into this new age.

Many of those controllers will probably find themselves pushing buttons and turning knobs on computers in the future, for the job of air traffic control still needs to be done, and computers will need human back-up. In the same way, pilots will no doubt find changes coming into their jobs. And the airlines? Well, some of them already have airplanes with the NASA-developed systems on order. How they compare in price to today's models, which still fly on human wits and muscle, is not yet known. But what is known is that airline and all other airborne traffic is going to go up by 50 percent in the next decade, so whenever the age of flight by computers dawns, it will be none too soon.

Epilogue

The story that follows has to do with safety in the air in the most elemental sense of the term. It was written more than 20 years ago, in my early years of flying, and I like to think that it will find some sort of an echo in the hearts of other pilots who may read it. For surely every pilot has known, at some time in his career aloft, this sort of basic confrontation between living and dying, when the choice of which it shall be belongs entirely to him and God. In this way, it also lays bare the quintessential heart of flying, which is this: it is as dangerous an occupation today as it was when the Wright brothers first launched us all into the skies. The difference is the training and skill and dedication of the men and women who make it as safe as it is. They have not changed the nature of flying, but they have greatly changed the practice of it.

None of them were with me that day 20 years ago, when I faced my ordeal. Or maybe they were with me in spirit, listening as I cruised around there in the darkening sky, but I could not hear them. I was alone, as every pilot is when his moment of truth comes. This is how it was, for me.

The field was a very ordinary looking one—ragged, tufted with bushes and thin sapling trees, unwanted, untended, obviously abandoned. I had probably seen it many times before, on earlier flights in my student pilot days when I was doing short cross-country runs from Teterboro Airport in New Jersey past the Kensico Reservoir to Bridgeport, Danbury, or the Westchester County Airport near White Plains. On such trips I played a little game, a useful game: flying along, I would study the ground below trying to pick out places where, in the unlikely event of an engine failure or other emergency, I might safely land. It helped to pass the time, it kept me on my toes and always well aware of where I was.

This field, however, even had I consciously seen it, would scarcely have attracted further study. It had no character; it hardly stood out from the surrounding landscape of woods, meadows, and low hills. Roughly rectangular in shape, it was bordered along its eastern edge by a line of spreading maples and a low stone wall which separated it from a small road. The western edge trailed off into thick scrub and brush. From the north, a wooded hillside sloped down toward it; to the south, it faded into nothingness. A tumbledown barn lay there, some bits of rusty junk, a clump of sumac growing wild in a hollow, nothing more. And on the field itself, the grass looked scrofulous from the air, with spreading brown patches eating away at its sparse green, like a middle-aged man growing bald.

I never would have picked it, I am sure.

It is eight o'clock of a beautiful, early summer day. We are at the airport in Allentown, Pennsylvania—my son Peter, whom I picked up from his Ohio college yesterday, his friend Jay, who is going home to Long Island, and I, three travelers in Tripacer 3212-Z-for-Zebra, a trim red-and-white ship waiting for us on the apron outside. The sun, already well up, promises a day of warmth and some humidity, but right now it is clear and fresh and cool, with only a thin gauze of high cirrus clouds 10,000 feet or more above. I have already checked the weather ahead. New York is spotty, with Idlewild reporting scattered clouds at 10,000 feet and visibility of ten miles; La Guardia, 5,000 scattered, visibility five miles with haze and smoke; and Teterboro, down on its industrial plain, 5,000 scattered and three miles with haze and smoke. We decide to make for Flushing, a neat, small field in the loom of mighty La Guardia and handy to the subway and home.

By nine o'clock we are ready. We climb in and settle down, I start the engine, turn to face the control tower, turn on the radio, and call Ground Control, which regulates the traffic on the runways, on the standard frequency of 121.9.

No answer.

"Funny," I think, "I've had no trouble on that frequency before." But Ground Control is tricky; often there are dead spots in the short distance between plane and tower, sometimes just depending on which way the plane is turned. I taxi a bit further out and try again: "Allentown Ground Control, this is Tripacer 3212-Zebra, visitors' ramp, ready to taxi. Over."

A four-engine DC-6 Mainliner rumbles past, its engines belching loudly in the quiet morning air. My radio, tune it as I may, is silent. But now I see a green light flashing at me from the Tower window. Ah! They have heard me; I am cleared to taxi to the runway. We swing around behind the huge four-engine job and follow it along, feeling very much like a dinghy obediently trailing the Queen Mary. At the head of the runway we both turn into the wind to run our engines up for a final check of instruments and magnetos.

Right behind us is another airliner, a Martin 202. The roar of his two big engines drowns us out completely as he revs them. Peter and Jay stare out in awe. The DC-6 ahead of us is ready: under full throttle now, he rolls, lifts, climbs, and disappears. It is our turn; I switch to Tower frequency and call: "12-Zebra, ready for takeoff".

No sound comes from my radio. No reply.

"Oh, for God's sake!" I think. "Not now! Not with all those passengers waiting in that monster behind me!" I switch quickly back to another frequency and try again. No answer. The two big engines behind me rev impatiently—the giant is clearing his throat, telling the pipsqueak to get going. Sweating slightly, I call again. "Allentown Tower, 12-Zebra, ready for takeoff. If you are reading me, please give me a green . . ."

Thank God, there it is! The tiny, bright green eye winks reassuringly at me from the window half a mile away. Just to make sure, I swing around quickly and scan the skies for any approaching planes; there are none. The runway comes around again as we complete the turn; without further ado, I shove the throttle all the way forward, the engine answers with a ringing peal of undisguised relief, and we are off at last.

As we square away on our course for home, I try the radio once more, tuning to the Allentown Tower frequency. With perfect clarity I hear the last words of their farewell exchange with the Martin 202, now climbing out behind us—a report of the weather at its destination. Well, it must have been some sort of ground effect after all.

After the trackless West Virginia hills of yesterday, the road home seems like a thruway in the sky. I have omnidirectional radio beacons ahead of me, behind me, and to either side. I tune in on an outbound leg of the East Texas range just behind us; the musical beeps and blips sound comfortingly in our little cabin. On course at 85 degrees, I am heading straight for Teterboro. From there I plan to cross the Hudson and sail out over the Bronx, well north of La Guardia's traffic pattern, coming into Flushing from the east, over Long Island Sound. Everything is hunky-dory: my checkpoints on the ground roll up right on time—Easton on the Delaware, then Hampton to our left, the river and the railroad track near High Ridge, and the first of the low hills that we must cross before we come out on the Newark plain.

Over these hills we meet the first of the predicted scattered clouds. Only they are not at 5,000 feet, as predicted, nor even at 3,000; they are right on our level, and we are flying at 2,500. I dodged a big one in the first line, ducking to the left then back again. The next line seems a mite thicker, and I trim the airplane for a slow descent to 2,000. The haze, too, is thickening—where before we could see 15 or more miles ahead, now we can see 8 perhaps 10. But this is as expected; the sky above is still clear blue, the sun shines brightly, and, with our engine humming sweetly, we fly happily on.

The houses below are thickening now; almost imperceptibly, villages and hamlets are merging into suburbs and towns. Ahead and slightly to the right, the broad plain of Newark opens up, a mighty stage set rolling into view. But there, where smoke from a thousand factories hangs over the marshes, it is ominously dark and gray, like an undissipated twilight. I push aside an old, familiar twinge of fear that this sight always raised in me—I hate low-lying haze, in which the world shrinks to the size of a teacup, a tiny circle just below the plane. "Let's forget Teterboro," I think; "we're not going there today anyway." Instead, I swing a few degrees to the left, where the haze is light and bright in the warm sun. We can hit the Hudson slightly higher up the line and avoid the mess down there.

Morristown comes up, a nice, inviting field, and I point it out to Peter, who is sitting beside me. "Remember it," I say. "Just in case." He nods. It's always wise to have someplace to go back to in case of need, and Morristown was good to me once when I got caught in an unexpected flurry of snow.

The marching lines of scattered clouds are closer together now, and thicker. They are also, I note with some trepidation, lower—we are at 2,000 feet and I am dodging occasionally to avoid brushing their tendriled bottoms. But the visibility is still good, five miles or more. Below us, the suburbs have merged into a continuous carpet of small houses, a crawling, multicolored conglomeration of life feeding into the great city that looms like a shadow to the east. A two-lane parkway appears, snaky with black lines of cars, then a great cloverleaf crossroad. We are coming up on Paterson, north of our original course but right where I want to be now. I relax a bit and peer ahead.

There the sky is condensing to a bright, milky white, with blue above. Light though it is, there is something vaguely sinister about it, like a too-bright smile. By comparison to that dark smog to the right it is inviting—but inviting to what? I have heard of neophyte pilots like myself who flew on into slowly thickening haze and found themselves, all at once and without warning, flying in a cloud . . .

We are on a line with Teterboro now—Teterboro, my home field. Teterboro had 5,000 feet and three miles visibility—make it 2,000 and three now; that's still good. I know exactly where the field is from here. Perhaps it would be better if . . . On a sudden impulse, I tune the receiver to 119.5, the Teterboro Tower frequency, switch the transmitter to 122.5, and call.

"Teterboro Tower." My voice seems muffled by the haze and the marching clouds. "Teterboro Tower, this is Tripacer 3212-Zebra. Over."

Silence.

I twist the little crank on the receiver, tuning back and forth over the 119.5 frequency on which they should reply. Suddenly a voice breaks in loudly: "Pan American so-and-so . . ." (I don't quite catch the figures) ". . . cleared for takeoff runway . . ." There follow in rapid sequence runway number, wind, altimeter setting, and a clearance to St. Louis or someplace far away.

That couldn't be Teterboro! Pan American doesn't fly out of there. It must be Idlewild on 119.1. I call again, asking Teterboro for a long count so that I can tune in on them precisely; then I listen, tuning anxiously back and forth over the dial.

Nothing. Silence. I call again, on another frequency. No replay.

And 12-Zebra drones along, into the slowly thickening haze.

I sit and think for a moment, trying to form a plan. No need to be scared yet; the skies ahead are still light, visibility is at least five miles, if not more. But I am worried now about trying for Teterboro, not knowing for certain if they have heard me. Conditions are certainly good enough for a landing, but what about an airplane, my airplane, blundering in there, appearing suddenly and unannounced in what may be a busy traffic pattern? I don't like that thought. I decide, for the moment, to fly on to the Hudson, then fly down along it to the George Washington Bridge, turning there to come in on the field from the east. That way, the wind being southwest (as I can tell from the smoking chimneys on the ground), I can arrive in proper fashion on the downwing leg of the traffic pattern and, keeping a sharp lookout, get close enough to blink my landing lights at the Tower in lieu of a radio contact.

But the Hudson offers no help. It comes up right on schedule, with its tall television tower that marks one end of the Teterboro flight schools' practice area, and it gleams silvery below us, a tug and barge etched sharply on its slightly crinkled surface. As I turn down it, however, I see that to the southward side it is veiled in thick, gray haze. I try it for a bit, cautiously, but I can't even see the bridge at three miles. I can, however, see two seaplanes winging down below the level of the Palisades, bright, cleanly outlined little toys on their long pontoons. They can land on the water if they have to. They go on, and as I turn away, I envy them with all the powerful emotion of the fear that now slowly, coldly crawls into my heart.

I turn and fly upriver once more. The haze is brighter still, and more opaque, but here I have at least three miles visibility; I still can see. And across the river, to the east, is Westchester County Airport, well clear of all the city's traffic, a place that I know well. I turn toward it and leave the Hudson behind. I give it one last look—it may still be an avenue of escape in case I need it, a way back to Morristown, or northward to Poughkeepsie. There is nothing critical yet in this situation; only the vagaries of the radio really worry me. I look ahead, peering intently into the soft, white brightness, waiting for familiar landmarks, which now assume an importance they never quite had before.

As we fly, I look up the Westchester tower frequency. Here it is: 118.5. I tune the receiver with utmost care. It must not fail me when I need it this time.

The New York Thruway floats by below, then another big highway, a town, a golf course. I know them all, and I turn slightly northward. I want to find the Kensico Reservoir: Westchester is just beyond its southeastern end. I must be about five miles out now. I pick up the microphone and call: "Westchester Tower, Tripacer 3212-Zebra. Over."

Silence. We fly on.

There is no time to fool around now. I switch the transmitter to 121.5, the emergency frequency. "Westchester Tower, this is Tripacer 3212-Zebra, coming up on the reservoir from the west. I am having trouble making radio contact. Will you give me a long count, please. Over."

I twist the handle slowly, carefully. I cannot hear them. *I cannot hear them!* I turn the volume up to full loud. Silence. We fly on.

Could I have the frequency wrong on my receiver? I check again: it is 118.5. I tune and get a blast of noise that stops as suddenly as it began. I call again: "Westchester Tower, Tripacer 3212-Zebra listening on 118.5. Would you give me a long count, *please*."

Nothing. Silence. We fly on. The doors are slowly closing on me; for the moment I don't know what to do.

Then, like the love-lit serenity of a welcoming face, like the cool breath of life on a fevered cheek, the reservoir slides into view.

This place I know like the backyard of my home. I grew up near here. Down there, where the aerating plant sends its dozens upon dozens of plumed sprays into the cleansing air, we used to picnic when I was a child. The Thousand Fountains, we used to call the place, and it has always remained one of my most vivid childhood images. I could follow the roads from here to the airport; we are almost home. My relief is so great that it very nearly brings tears to my eyes. And I raise them, and I look ahead, and my heart grows cold as stone.

Haze curtains the hills on the far side of the reservoir, a haze no longer milky, but gray. It hangs on those wooded crests, right to the treetops, and there are clouds above. The road ahead of me is closed, irrevocably.

I put the Tripacer into a steep left turn, and now I see what I have so often heard about and feared. It is the classic situation: behind me, the soft gate of haze and cloud have swung, too. The trap is shut; I am caught here, 1,500 feet above the reservoir with no place where I can go.

I steal a glance at Peter beside me. He is staring out into the haze-hung heavens, fascinated. He does not know, nor does his friend sitting there so trustingly behind me. The knowledge is mine alone. I am the pilot, for this I trained, for this I flew those many hours, learning, so that at this moment, alone with my knowledge, I would know what to do.

Fear is something that rides with a pilot always, a steady and expected companion. Fear enters the airplane gently, unobtrusively but positively, as the pilot swings his ship onto the runway and, in the last instant before decisive action, looks down that long expanse whence he will lift into another world. Fear is there as he shoves the throttle forward, watching intently, heightening his senses, sharpening memory and reflexes as the aircraft, feeling the first

145

slippery grip of wind upon its wings, strives toward its element. And fear relaxes as, airborne, the plane leaves the ground and climbs into the limitless sky. Fear is the pilot's friend, prodding him with little jabs of consciousness as he wings his often monotonous, sometimes soporific way through the lonely skies; alerting him, as he nears his destination, to the urgencies of coming safely back to earth again; riding with him, reminding him always of the alien qualities of this element that he has entered and that tolerates him for his skills alone. Yet fear can turn, in an instant, from a friend into the pilot's mortal enemy, paralyzing will and action if he lets it get the upper hand.

Such fear knows no reason, only a blind instinct for survival; and it is such fear that, very briefly, I know now. I am circling familiar ground: I see it with an unnatural clarity, a brilliant focus— it is so near! It almost seems that if I just let go, just close my eyes, the nightmare will be over, I will be down. For just that briefest instant I am a child again: I want to be home . . .

. . . And in the same instant, reason and training reassert themselves. Reason tells me that what I really have to fear is panic; to panic would be the worst thing that could happen to me now. There are two lives aloft with me beside my own, one of them that of my own son, the other one of parents who have entrusted his life to me. I can ride with fear; but I must conquer panic; I must hold on to reason.

I cannot risk those hills. I do not have the skill to cope with clouds, to keep my plane upright and flying straight if I lose my horizon, my sense of up and down, my vital equilibrium. Forcing a cloud has killed many a pilot who could not fly by instruments alone. But I do not need to lose myself in that gloomy haze ahead. Even if I can top those hills, even if I can assume that Westchester County Airport has visibility and ceiling sufficent for approach and landing, which I cannot, I will not risk blundering into its traffic pattern just as I would not risk appearing suddenly and unannounced at Teterboro. And so I keep on circling and keep on flying. I do not call the field again. Instead, I go back to fundamentals: I concentrate on keeping my airplane in the air.

We circle, and I fly and think and reason. And then, this time quite calmly, as though inevitably, I know what I must do. I must go down. With that, my fear relaxes, and utter concentration takes over.

Landing an airplane, any airplane, anywhere, is a matter of orderly, almost mathematical procedure coupled with skills that, by unending repetition, become an instinct. It is a maneuver beautiful to contemplate and execute, like a perfectly drawn curve that, at its end, merges imperceptibly with the ground at which it aims. It follows a well-defined, tried and tested pattern: a rectangle around the landing place, upwind to check the field, crosswind to check for wind drift, downwind to the so-called key position from which the pilot knows that under all circumstances he can land the plane, then base leg, and final approach. The pilot, flying this pattern as he reaches toward the ground, performs functions that are automatic: he slows the plane; trims it for the most efficient glide; checks instruments, carburetor heat, mixture, tanks, controls. The airplane is obedient to his hands because it is an airplane, a machine built to fly. Properly flown, it will glide right to the ground where, at the final instant, under the pilot's careful hands, it will lose its flying speed and touch down. It is an inevitable process; only a shaky mind and shaky hands can confuse and throw it off its predetermined course, and I am going to make extremely sure that my mind and hands are steady now.

I have assets, priceless ones: I can see for at least two miles around my landing place; I have an utterly trustworthy airplane, known for its ability to land and take off almost anywhere; I have an engine beating strongly, an engine I can put my faith in. I have three hours of gas left in my tanks; I can circle here that long if necessary to make up my mind. I have wings and power and time—time to find a field, to plan my approach to that field, to think it out, search it out in every detail, and finally put her down.

And so I concentrate, unthinkingly, automatically, on the basic things: on keeping my plane aloft and finding a place to land.

The first thing that leaps into my field of vision is the Thousand Fountains. Here is a wide, grassy area on the banks of the reservoir. A pumping station blocks the northern end of it; then come the fountains themselves, shimmering in the weak sun that still shines through the haze on this small piece of earth that is now my personal world. Beyond them is a wide, clipped lawn, traversed by concrete roadways. One cuts across from east to west, the other runs almost straight, bordered by grass, toward a clump of pines at the far end, where it disappears toward the dam.

I study the area carefully. I could come in very low and touch down on that grassy border right beside the longer road. With full flaps and a full stall landing, I would come to earth at perhaps 55 miles per hour. If no cars were in sight, I might even land on the concrete. The run to the trees is short, but I just might make it.

I go through my landing checklist carefully. Mixture is on full rich, tanks are switched to fullest tank, carburetor heat is on. I reduce power, trim up, and 12-Zebra slows to 90 miles per hour. I put on first flaps and turn into my downwind leg.

Downwind! It hits me in the pit of the stomach. Which way is the wind, the vital wind?

Frantically, I study the ground below. I see no smoke, no telltale sign to tell me. I put an iron clamp on fear. How can I tell which way the wind is blowing?

The place I have picked faces south. All the way up, the wind has been from the southwest. It could hardly have changed here and now. And then I think of the water below. I study it carefully as we skim along, 800 feet above it. There is barely a crinkle on it. No wind is better than tailwind; if there is any wind, it must be southwest or south. I proceed according to plan.

I have a thought, then, for my passengers. I nudge Peter and point to the Thousand Fountains. "Down," I say. "I'm going down."

He stares back at me uncomprehendingly. I fly on.

A mile beyond my landing point I turn on my base leg. This has to be good, now. I watch my airspeed, that critical indicator of how I am flying. It shows 80 miles per hour as I turn. Too slow! I drop the nose, put on a little power, watch it come up to 85. I crane my neck to the left to see how my turn will come out.

There they are: the pumping station, the fountains, the concrete road, the grassy border. We sink toward it slowly. We are coming in fine. It looks almost like a regular runway. My hand reaches for the flap handle to apply full flaps—then jumps back to the throttle. Full power! We roar upward again, into the hazy sky.

My runway is no runway. It is an embankment, sloping steeply down from the road, a trick of the eye from aloft, a mirage.

But now, as I circle again, I see the field.

I believe now, looking back on everything that happened, that it was inevitable that I should try the Thousand Fountains first. A pilot *in extremis,* looking for a place to land, will pick the one that has the most familiar aspects—and the most familiar one to me was something that looked like a runway. The Thousand Fountains did—the concrete road, the grassy strip that bordered it—and so I went for that. But I do not try again, even for the chance of landing on the roadway. For I have seen the field.

It lies there on its hilltop, long, rectangular, barren and wasted in appearance, scrofulous with its balding spots of brown. But once I see it, it holds my eyes. It looks vaguely familiar, and suddenly I realize why: it is very like a field on Martha's Vineyard which, months before, my friend, instructor, and wise man beyond telling, Steve Gentle, pointed out to me as a likely place to land. We had even made a pass at it, with throttle closed, while Steve pointed out to me how I could probably steer between the low shrubs that speckled it here and there and, at the worst, get away with a few dents and scratches.

There it lies, as though it were waiting for me.

I study it with utmost care. I circle it twice, perhaps 100 feet above it, looking for its every mark and flaw.

I will have to come in from the north, over the low hill. That is no problem; but it is narrowest at its northern end. The grass is mostly brown and sere, in hummocks, but there are no rocks that I can see. There is a clump of bushes; I can skim those, setting down just beyond. After this, there are only isolated saplings. I can avoid most of these, I think, and if I hit a couple, they are not big enough to do any damage, certainly not enough to throw the plane off course. And there is plenty of room, plenty of room beyond.

This field, as I study it—this barren piece of abandoned land—becomes a Garden of Eden to me. It grows green and beautiful beyond description in my eyes, green with the promise of life. It is haven, it is home. There we will land, and in this airplane I know that I can do it.

I skim it one more time, the last time. Flying upwind, I check it end to end. I see the little houses across the road that borders it; there we will go after landing to knock on some door, to speak to people on the ground. Earth, earth! It never was so fair, so infinitely desirable. Like a vessel caught by storm, we have sighted port; it only remains now for us to get in.

I climb out past the lower boundary, turn, and swing into my downwind leg. I motion to Peter: "That's where we're going," and point to the field. "You mean we're going to land?" he asks, incredulous. "Yes," I reply. "We can get in there. Tighten your seat belt, now. Tell Jay."

"Holy smoke!" is all he says. "What a ball!"

Eight hundred feet above the reservoir we fly. This will have to be the most precise, the most careful landing I have ever made. We pass the northern boundary of the field and fly on. Well beyond it, I turn 12-Zebra onto our base leg, then onto final.

There it is. It is a field like any other, but it is mine. I line it up and cut the power. The engine dies to a steady murmur, at 85 miles per hour I check the glide and hold unwaveringly for the line of trees.

Down we come. We are too high. Right rudder, left aileron—the Tripacer obediently goes into a steep sideslip, losing height fast. Enough. Controls to neutral; back she comes to a straight glide. She is in firm control; 12-Zebra is flying like a searing gull and my heart warms to her. The hill flashes past below. A little power now; the trees are close. Full flaps! She balloons and then sinks. The trees come up, then disappear. The ground rises steeply before my eyes. Back on the wheel now! Flare and float! A quick glance at the airspeed—60 miles per hour and going down. Up comes the field before my eyes. It is a familiar sight! Yet it is so unfamiliar, with its brown grass, its shrubs where no shrubs should be!

Back on the wheel! Hold her off, hold her off! Her speed is dying; she floats along. She skims the clumpy grass. She touches. She is down. A shrub flashes up at me, a shrub I cannot avoid. Grass flies, there is a whistling rattle as the spare branches strike the wing. Then we are rolling, rolling over the old and worn-out earth that cannot sustain life anymore but has received ours; rolling and rumbling and cutting grass but holding rocklike steady on our tricycle gear.

We are down. We are safe beneath the sky. We are home.

I have an idiotic conviction that I must park the airplane. We could stop anywhere, but long training in the proper procedures still has me in its grip. And so we taxi, rumbling over the clumpy earth while the grass flies, down to the far end of the field. There I swing in, in approved fashion, lining 12-Zebra up square to the spreading maple trees, the stone wall, the road, and the houses beyond. I cut the engine. The world is suddenly very still. I hear a dog bark, an automobile horn sound. It is a warm summer day in a field beside the reservoir, and we are down.

What do I know now about that field? I know now that until about ten years ago it received and dispatched airplanes. I did not know it when it beckoned to me mutely from the earth, so near and yet so distant in that hour of test and travail; but I know now that it was once called Reynolds Field and that it was an airport, if only a small one, for many years. Was it that which called to me, after I abandoned the smooth grass and inviting concrete of the Thousand Fountains?

Fliers who once landed there will know it and remember it. When it was closed and abandoned, a decade ago, it subsided into nothingness; it turned barren, devoid of life, useless, but it lived on in the memories of some, and it was there for me. It took 12-Zebra and her passengers to its heart and welcomed them, and if it left her one small scar, a dent in the left stabilizer from the shrub I could not miss, I like to think it left that for memory's sake.

It welcomed us, and let us go again. That was my final memory of my field, when that same afternoon, in the hands of a pilot from Westchester County Airport, her dented stabilizer temporarily repaired, 12-Zebra took wing again and soared from the clump grass of long ago, back to the modern world. She got off in what seemed like no distance at all, and climbed into the clearing skies, leaving the field abandoned once again.

But on my maps it is marked forever: Reynolds Field.

Index